Copyright©2019 by Breece A. Perry

Photography & Illustration Copyright©2019 by Breece A. Perry

All rights reserved.

Other than excerpts for purpose of review, no works within this publication are to be used separately without explicit permission, reproduced or sold in part or whole profit.

HoneyBee Books:

<u>Artist, Photographer, Book Design</u>
Breece A. Perry

<u>Editor</u>
Breece A. Perry

<u>Producer</u>
Melissa L. Perez

First Edition October 2019

Introduction

Please refrain from turning another page unless you are 18 years or older.

These three books have been a wonderful project for me. I really enjoyed turning page by page through many old sketchbooks reminiscing while looking at these drawings from the last thirty years. These were the times and events in my life that were motivational enough to put down on paper. Thank you everyone for all the support with the first two books.

This is the third book in the series, the follow up to Breece Loses His Markers. This book will contain pencil, color pencil, color markers, black and white. All having the same focus on the THC counter-culture, not the mainstream that is has become recently. Yet, still not appropriate for many viewers. This will be a compilation of sketches, color, and incomplete. All will have a THC & Alcohol sub-culture heavily influenced, alternative mindset put to paper. These illustrations are an eclectic collection from a secret stash. If you enjoyed the first two books then you will really enjoy this one. Grab what ever gets you through the day. Get comfortable and enjoy turning through these fifty pages.

All drawings are done with pencil, ink, color markers and color pencils.

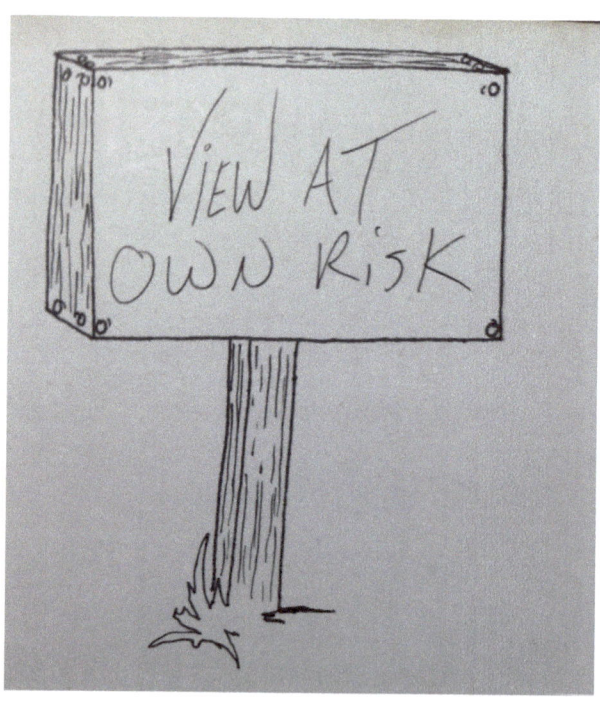

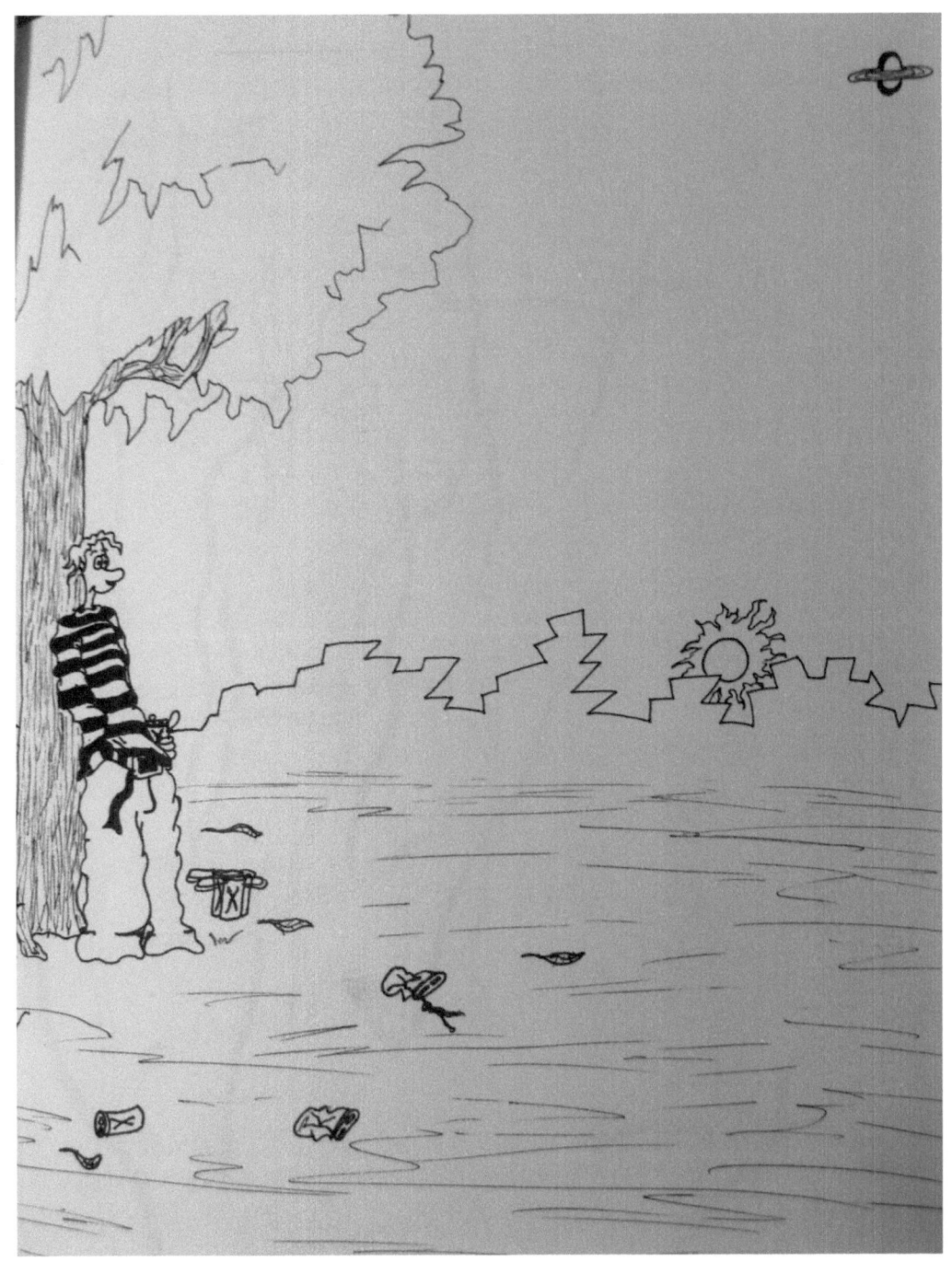

Sun, Downed a Sixer — 1989 — 8 inches x 11 inches

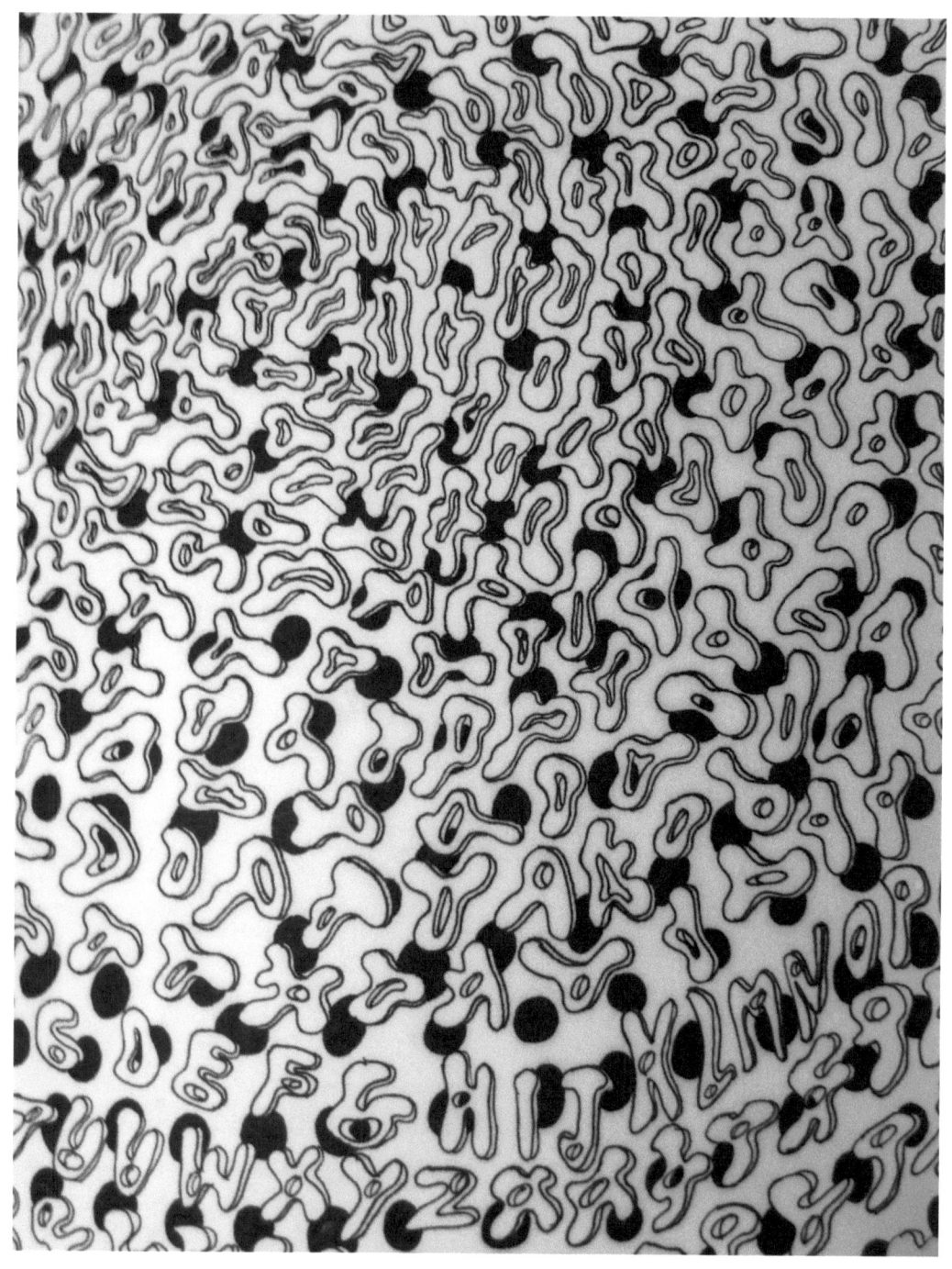

Learning the Alphabet   1989   8 inches x 11 inches

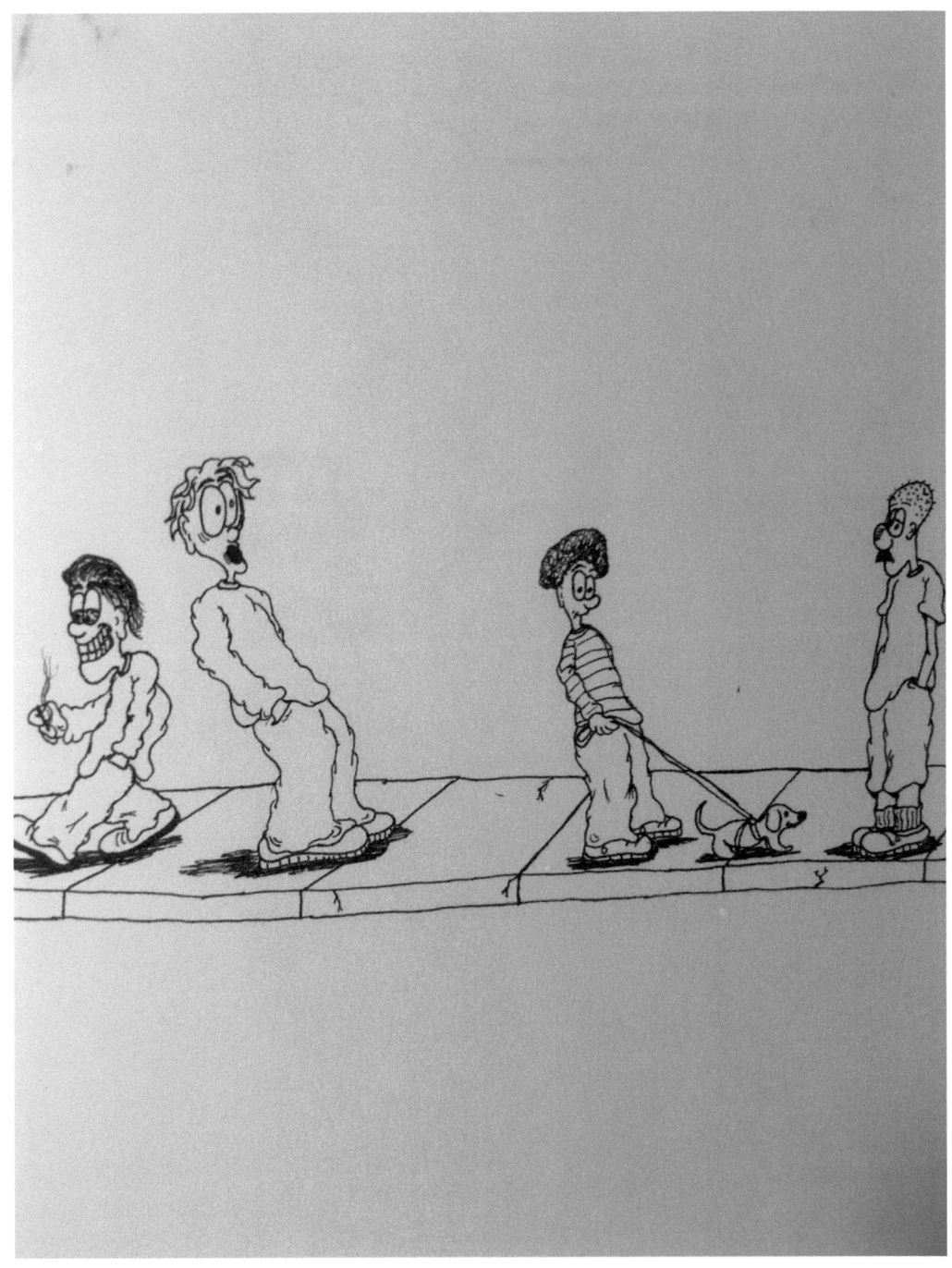

Out in Public   1989   8 inches x 5 inches

These next five images were from an early sketch book that was damaged. I cut out most of the drawings in the 1990s and placed them into a photo book to preserve the illustrations. The photo book has that tacky plastic page to hold photos in place. This gives the photo a weird light reflection and a strange background. A way to keep the drawings from any further damage.

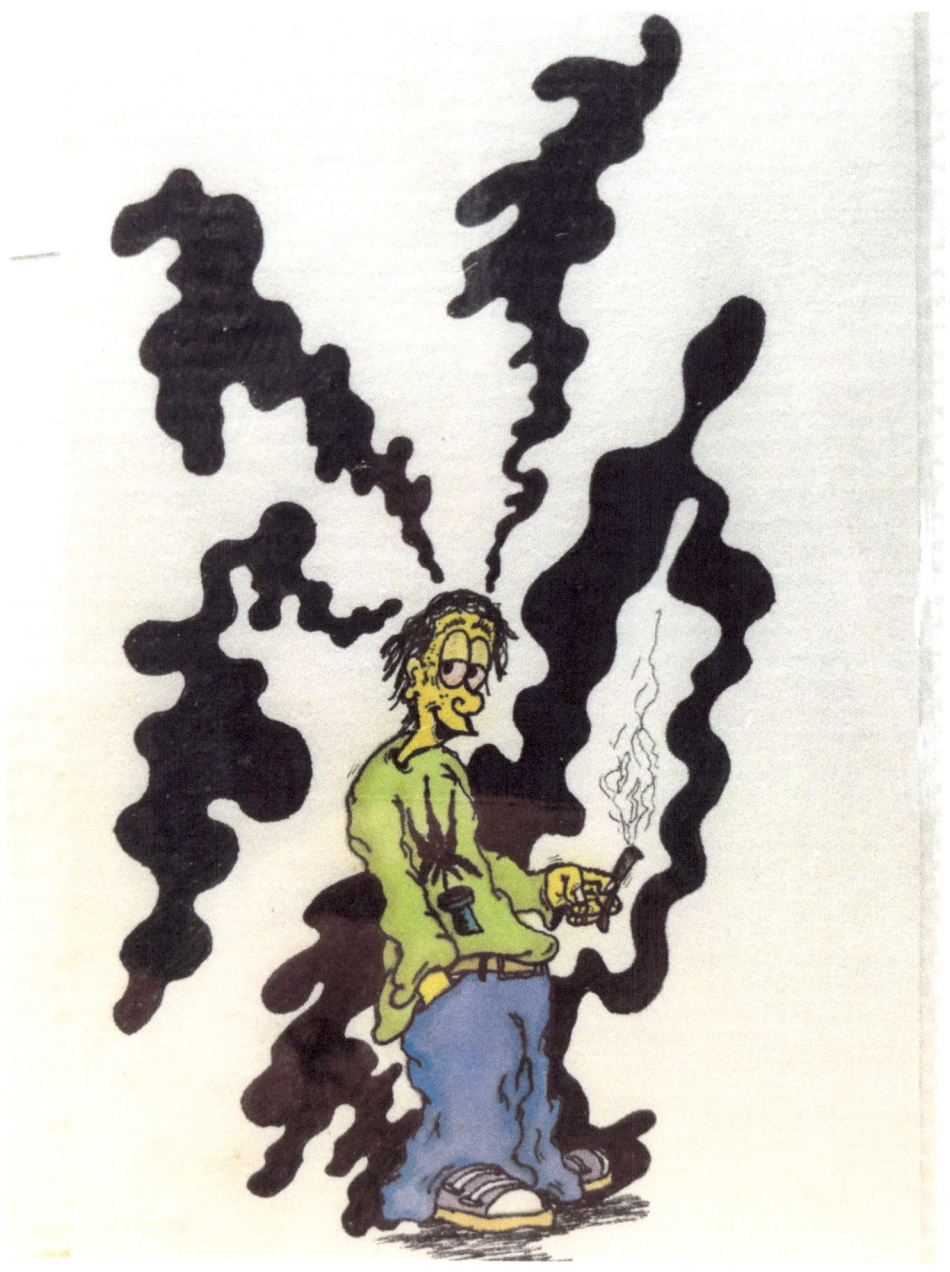

*Nice   1989   4 inches x 6 inches

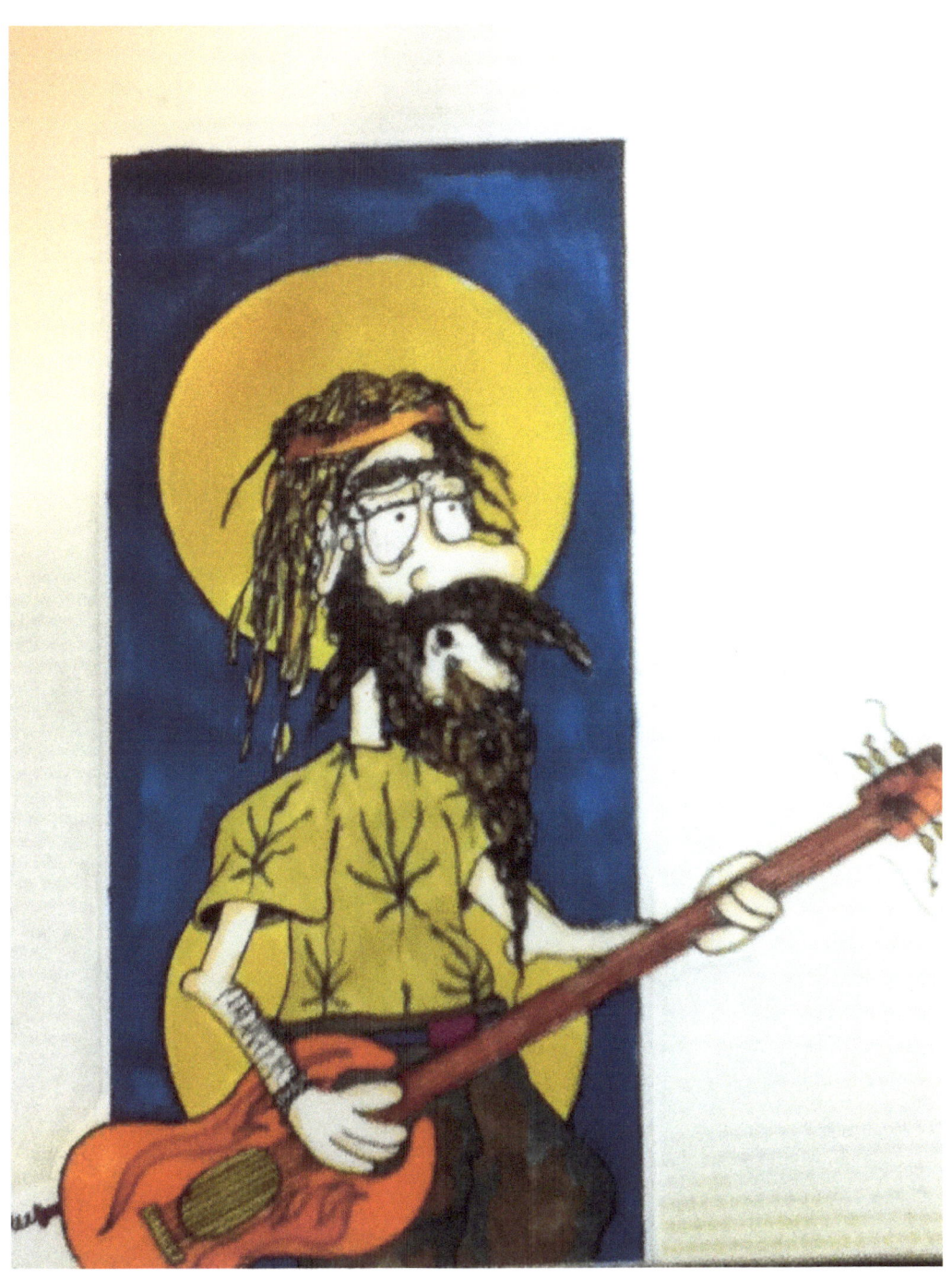

*Hippy Metal   1989   7 inches x 7 inches

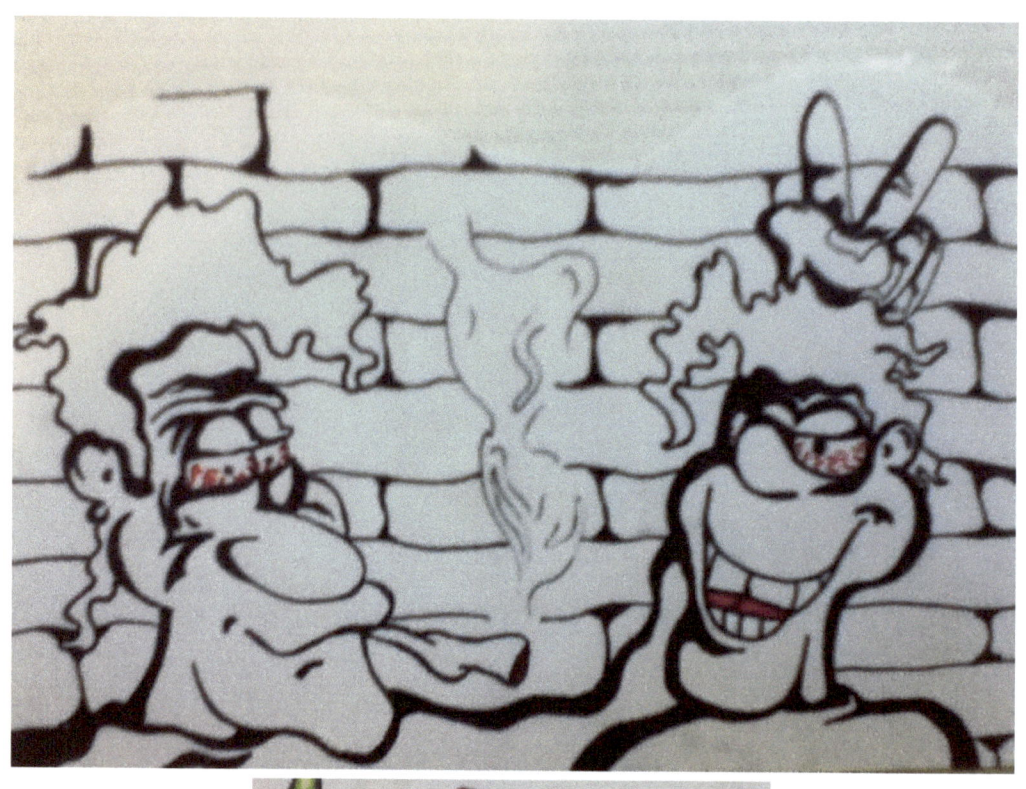
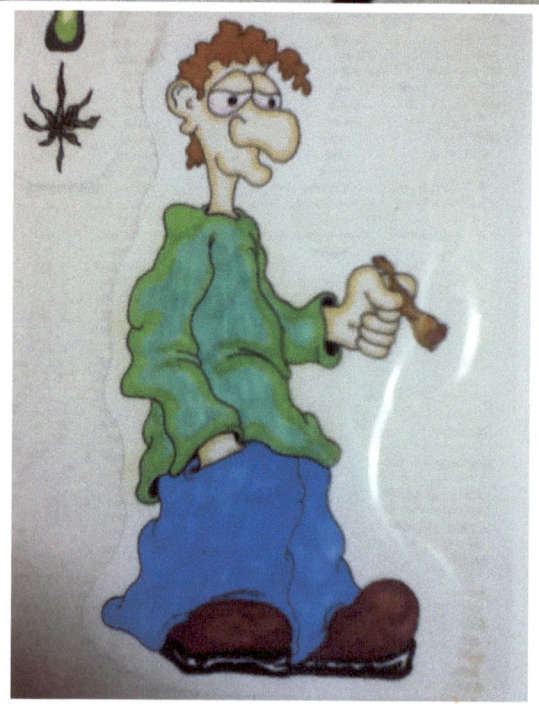

*The Red Eye (top)   1989   6 inches x 4 inches
*Probably 4:19 (bottom)   1989   3 inches x 6 inches

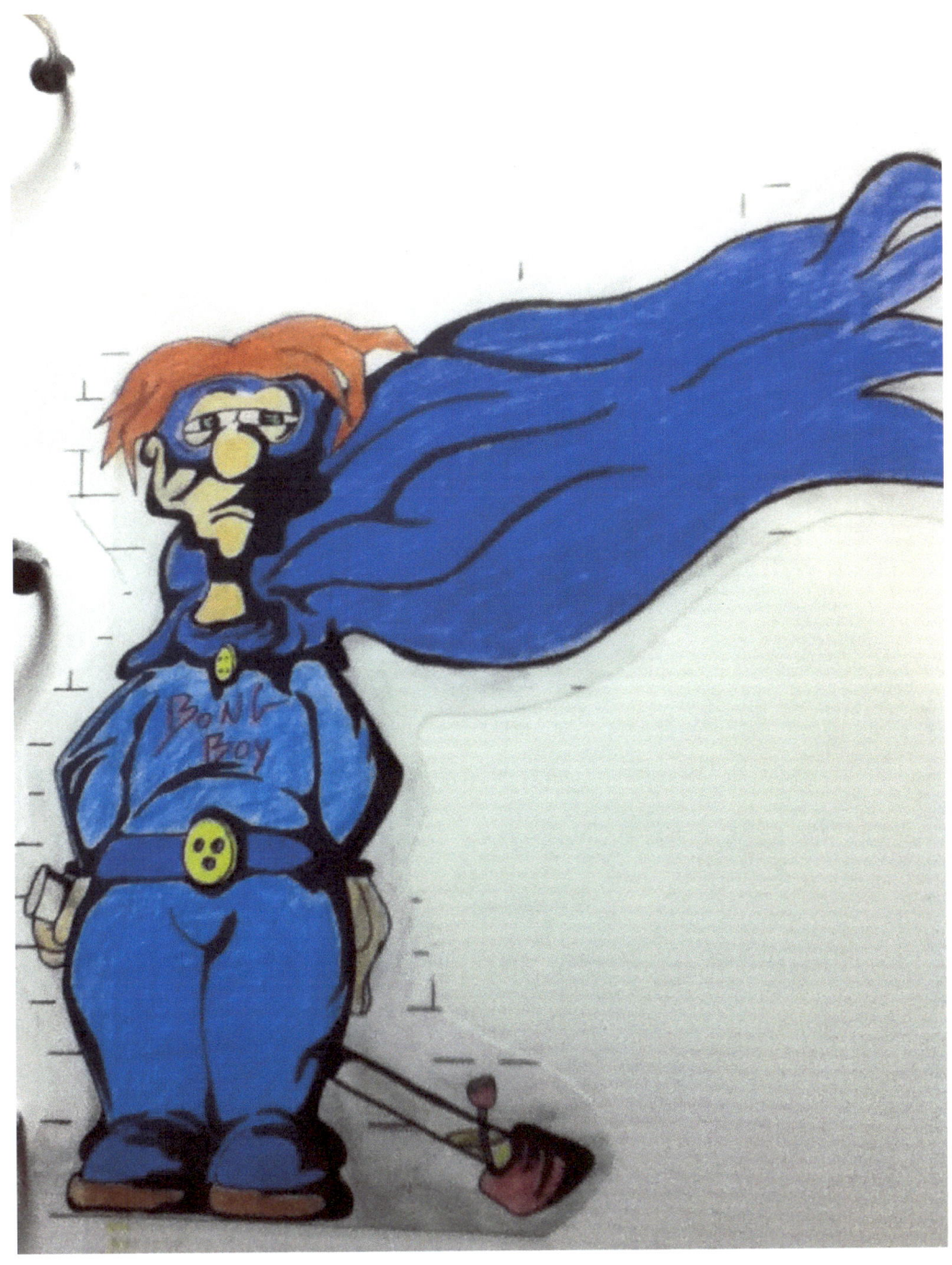

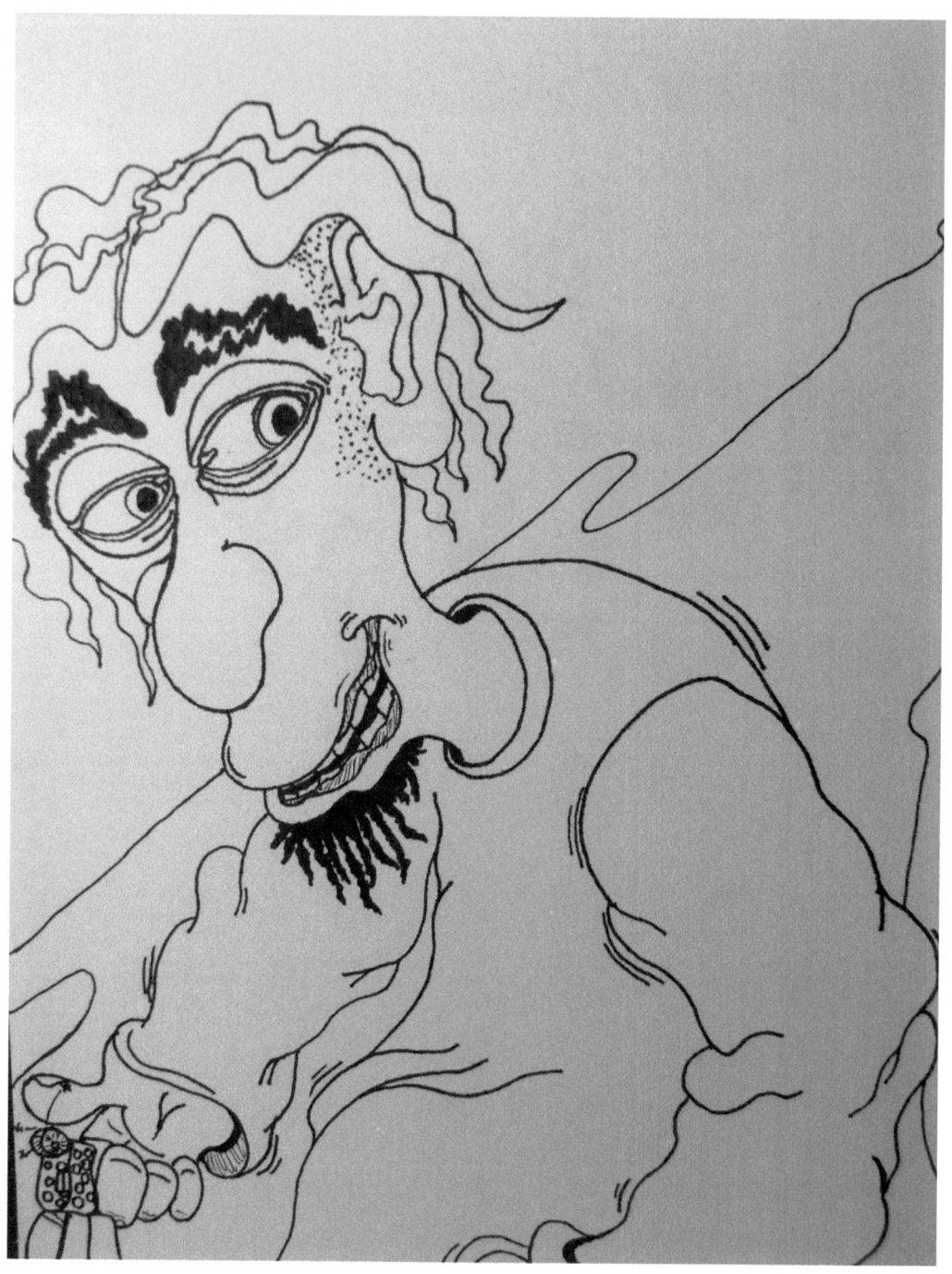

Trench Lighter   1989   6 inches x 9 inches

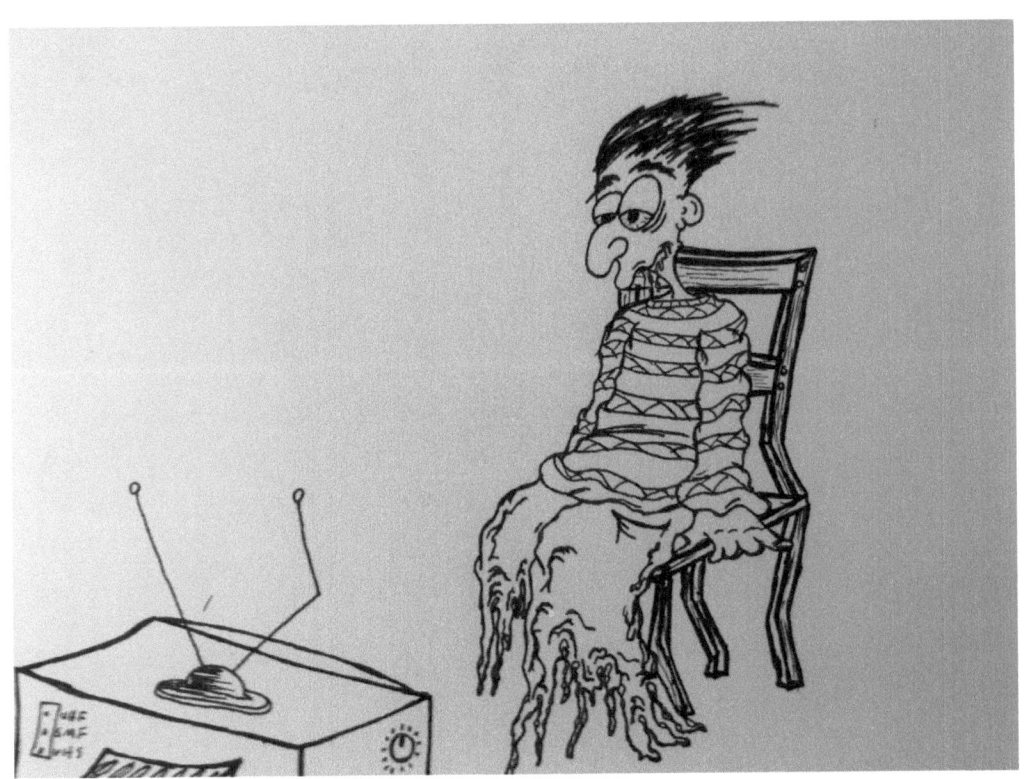

Broken Ankle   1989   9 inches x 6 inches

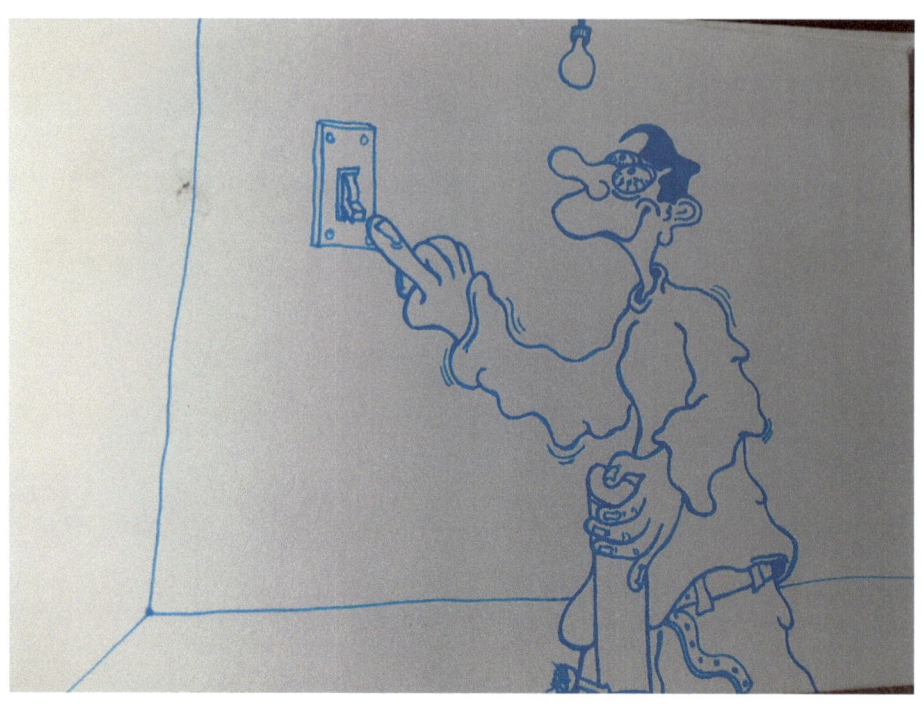

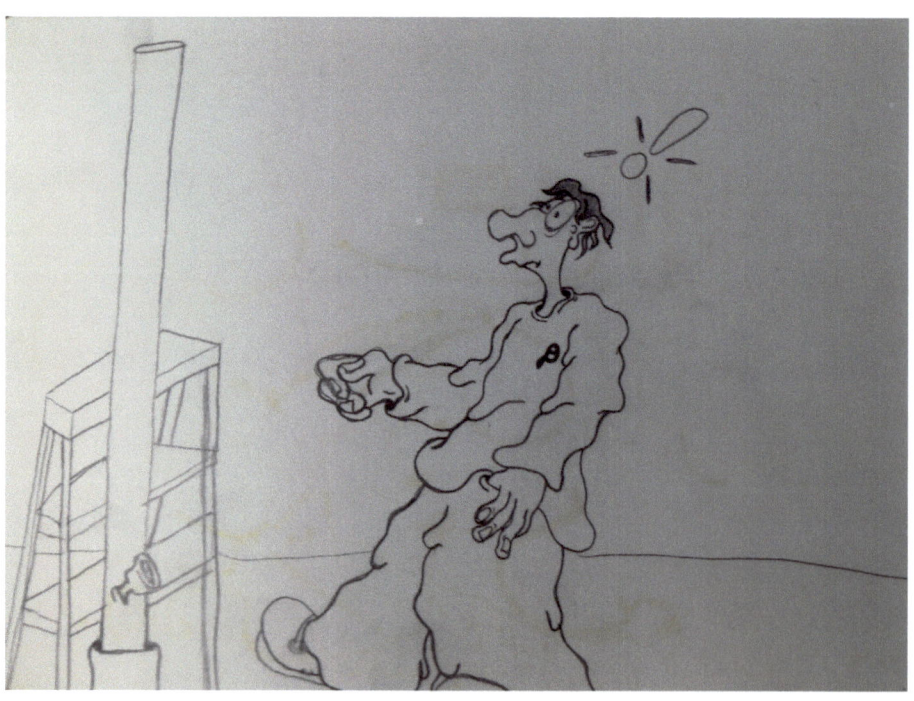

Black Light and Blue   (top)   1989   9 inches x 6 inches
Need a Teammate   (bottom)   1989   9 inches x 6 inches

Little did I know at that time in 1990 that in 1996 I would be heading out West. I have always been amazed by desert wildlife. I moved back out West in 2002 and mountain biked a lot. There were many interactions good and fearful out in the wilderness. I would recommend traveling coast to coast by road or even slower across America. It's not about the destination, it's about the journey!

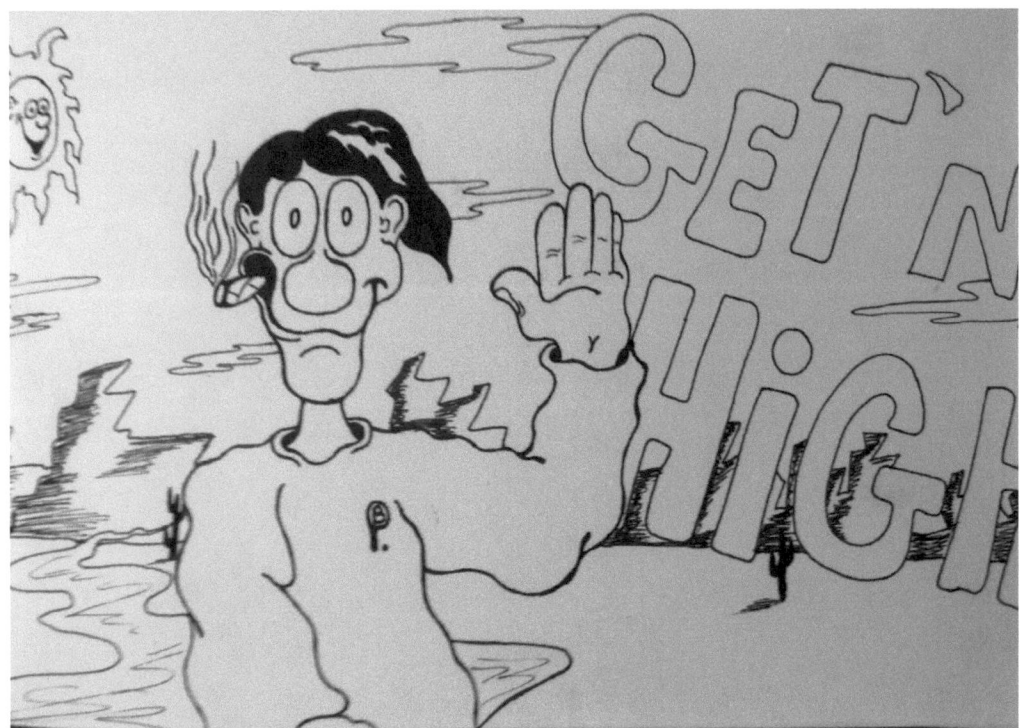

Get'n High   1990   9 inches x 6 inches

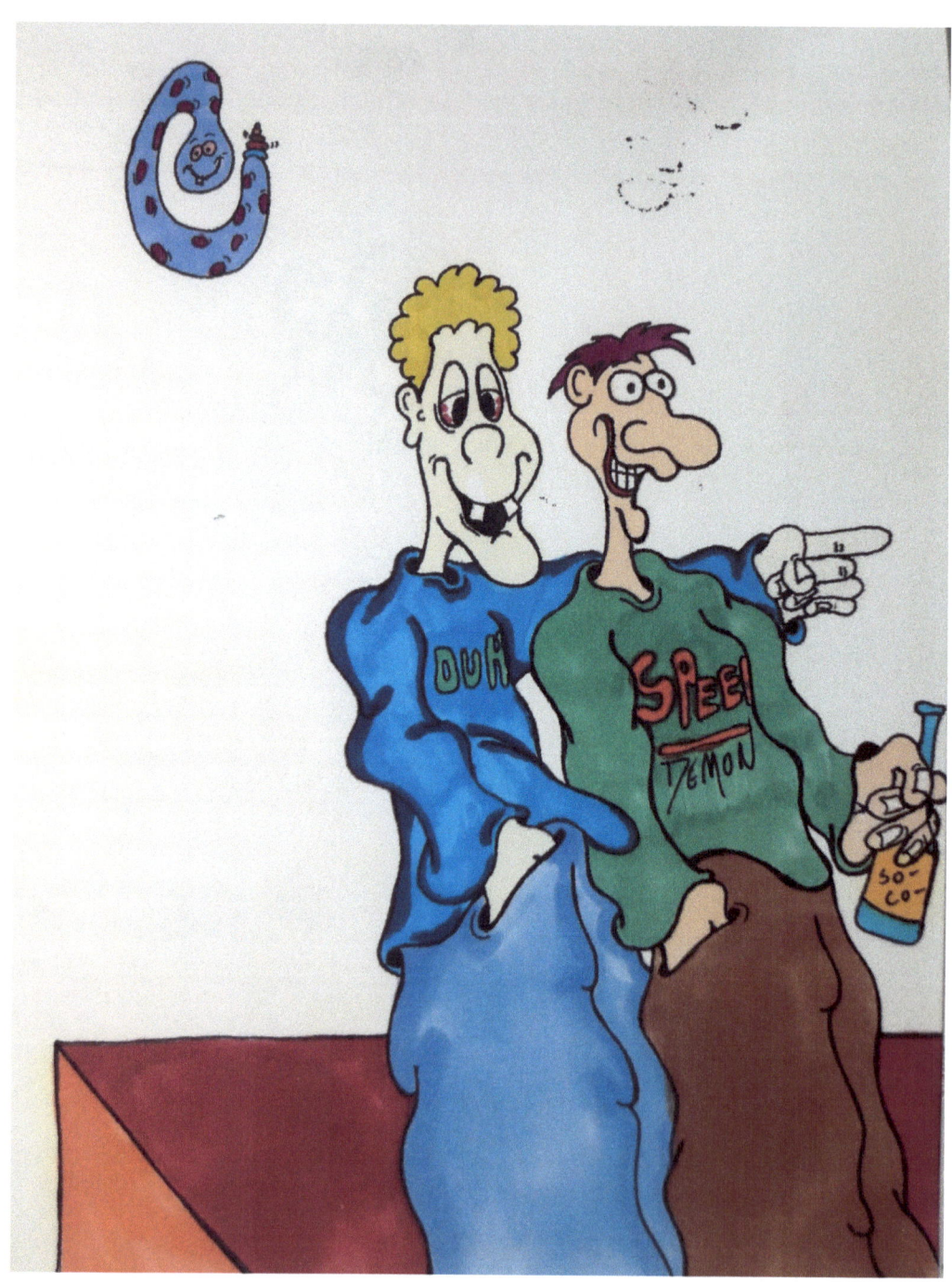

Lets Hang Out   1990   6 inches x 7 inches

This character is a doodle I have done over and over. Bob Dot is on many borders, bottoms and backs of most of my lined paper school notes. This has been a favorite character to draw over the years. A foundation of my drawing style. Either way Bob Dot always makes me laugh.

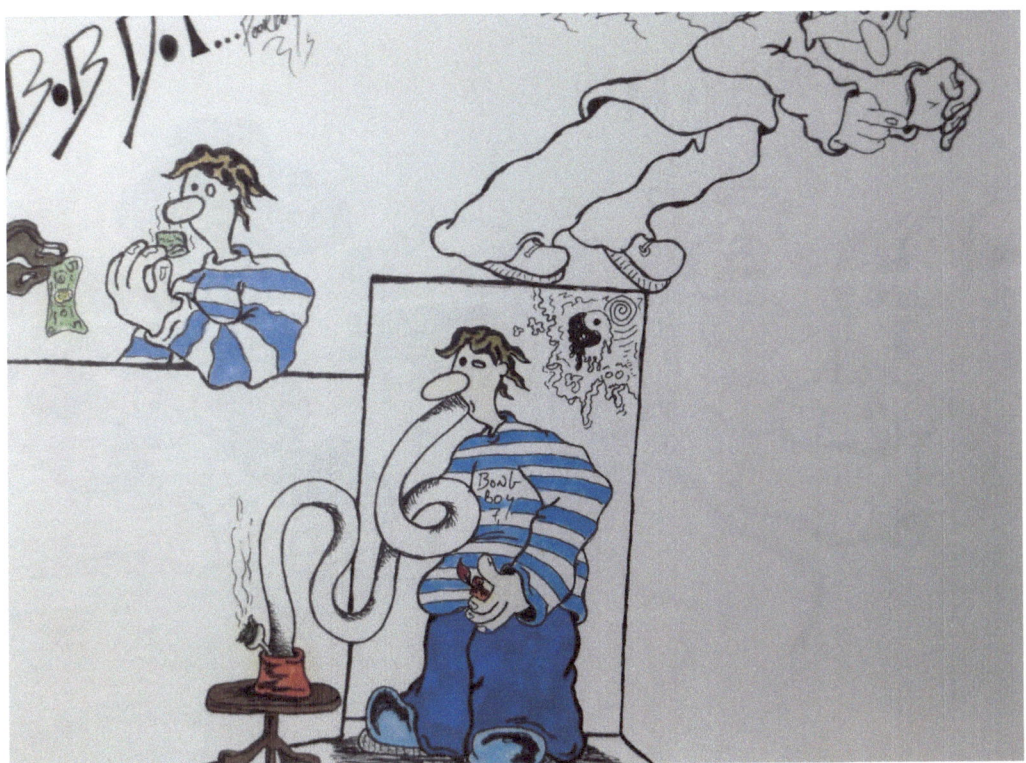

Bob Dot Feeling Blue   1990   9 inches x 6 inches

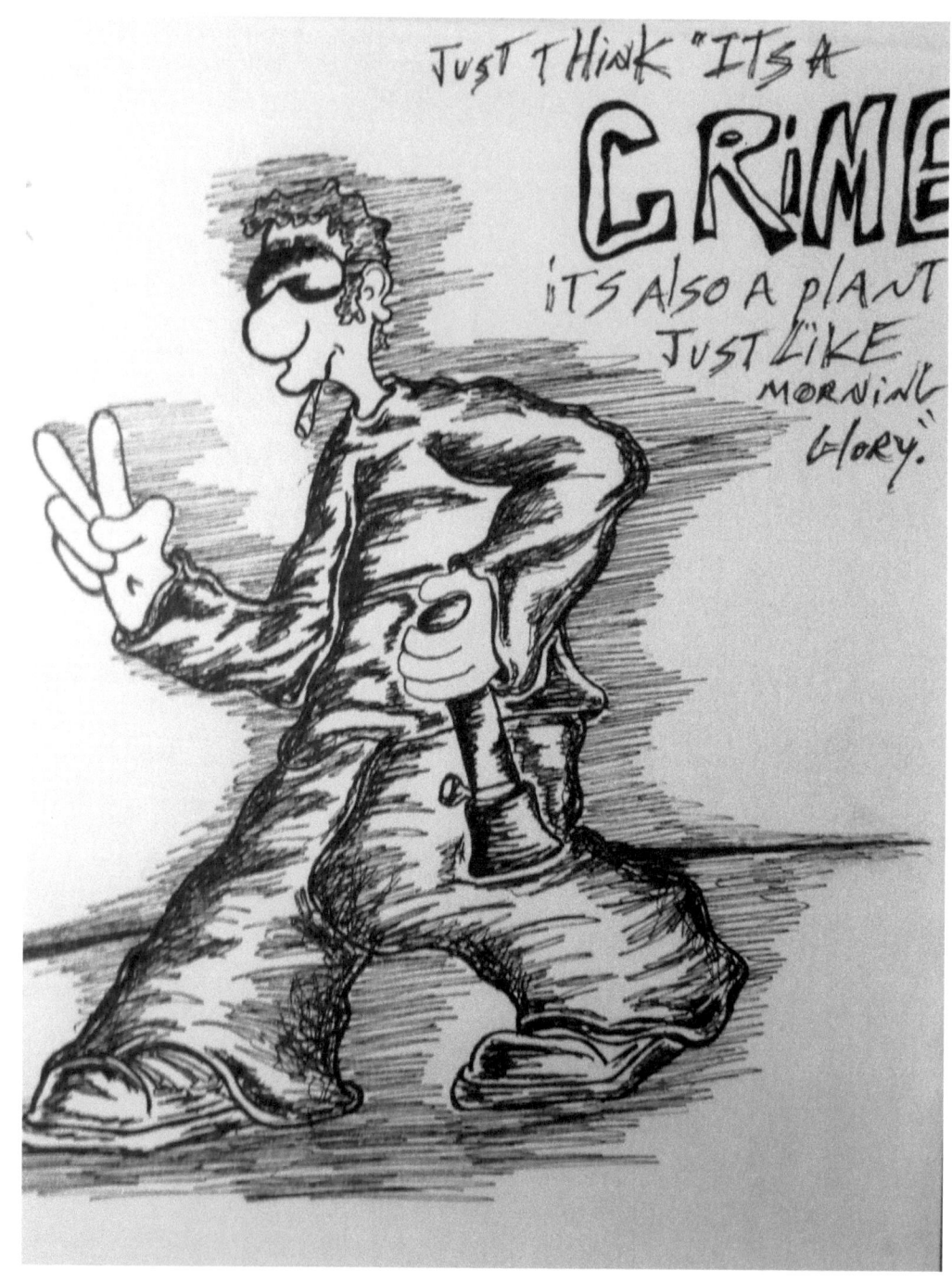

Morning Glory   1992   6 inches x 6 inches

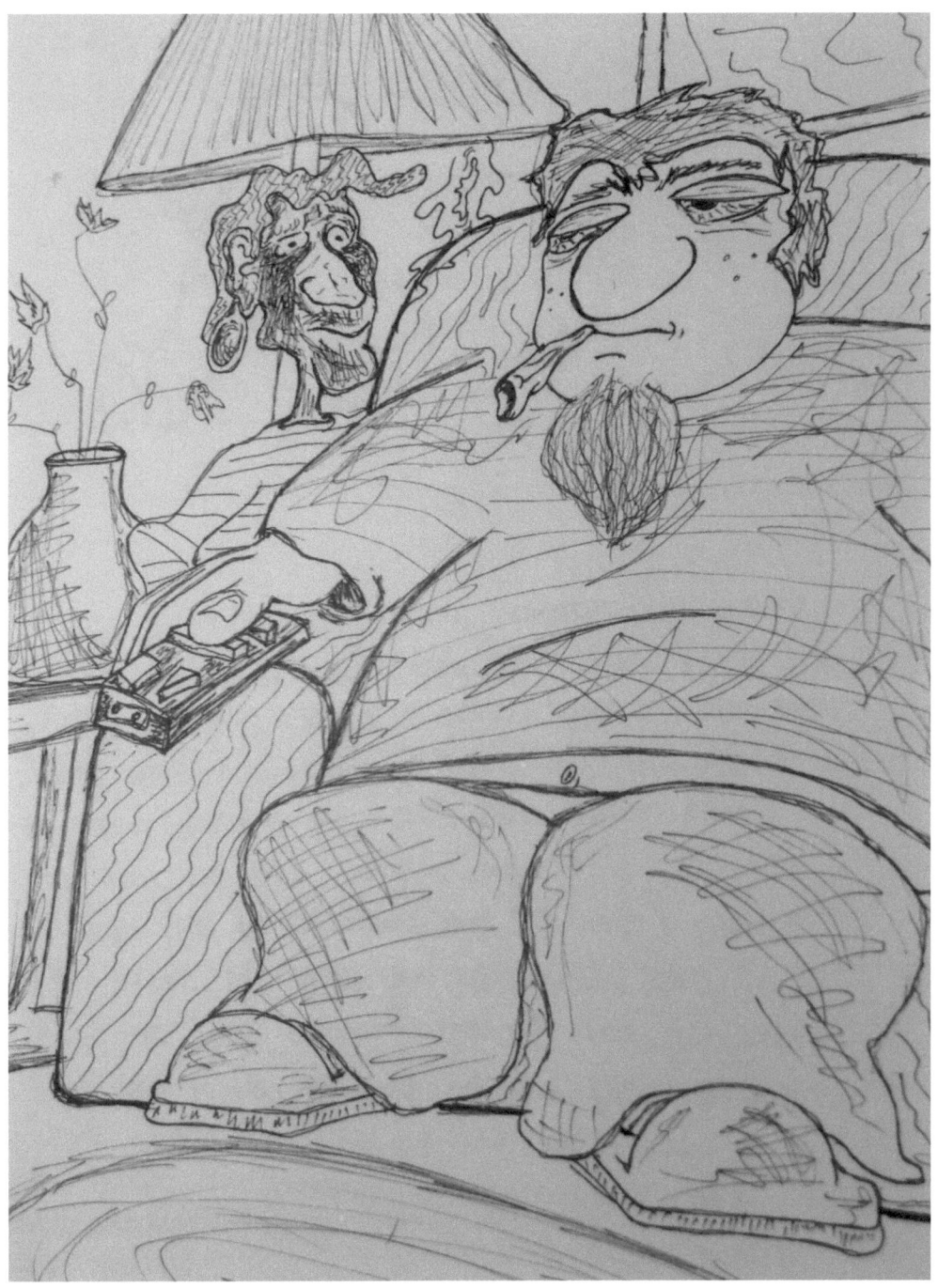

New TV Remote 1993 6 inches x 10 inches

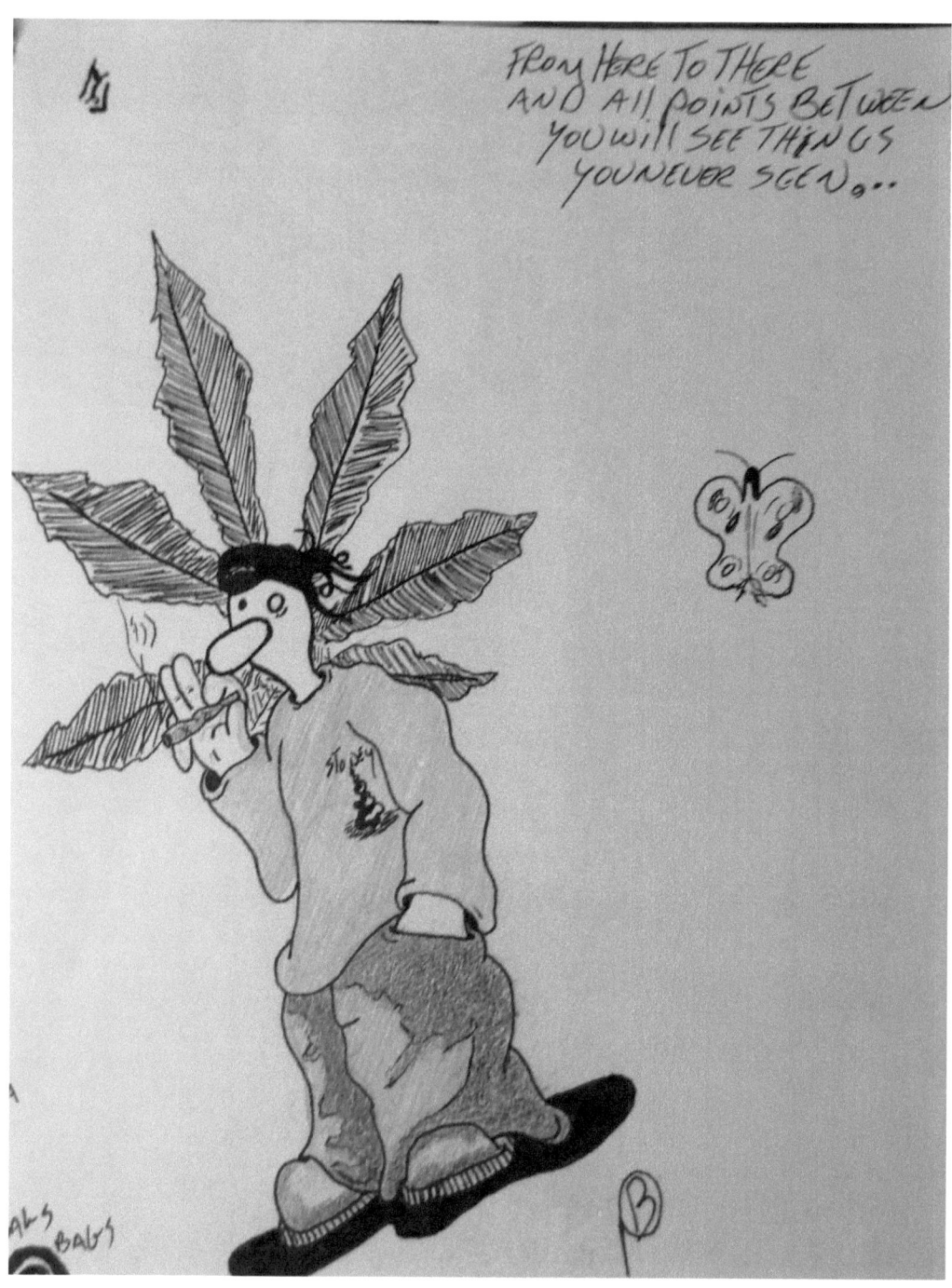

Stoned Solid Grey — 1993 — 5 inches x 7 inches

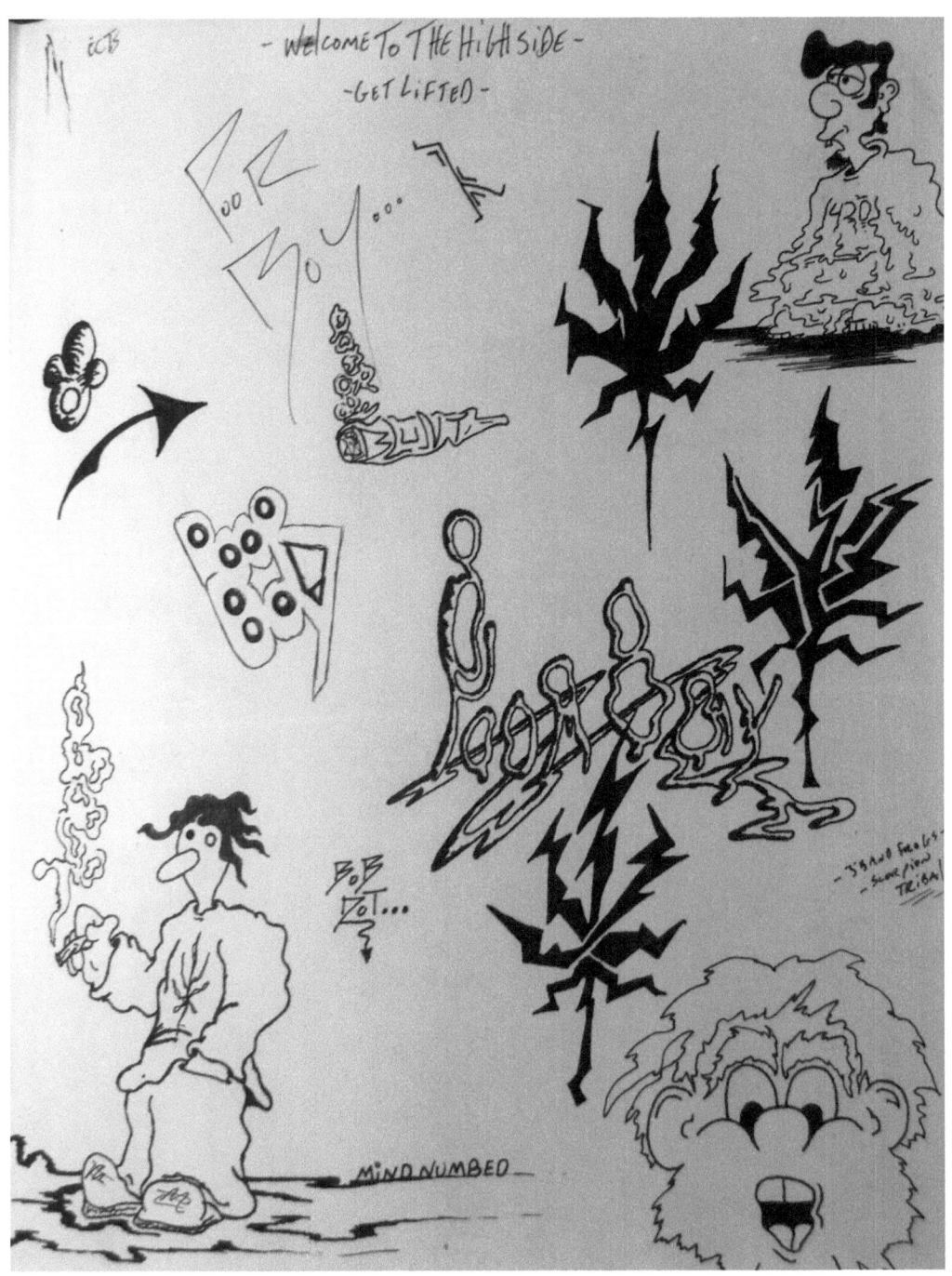

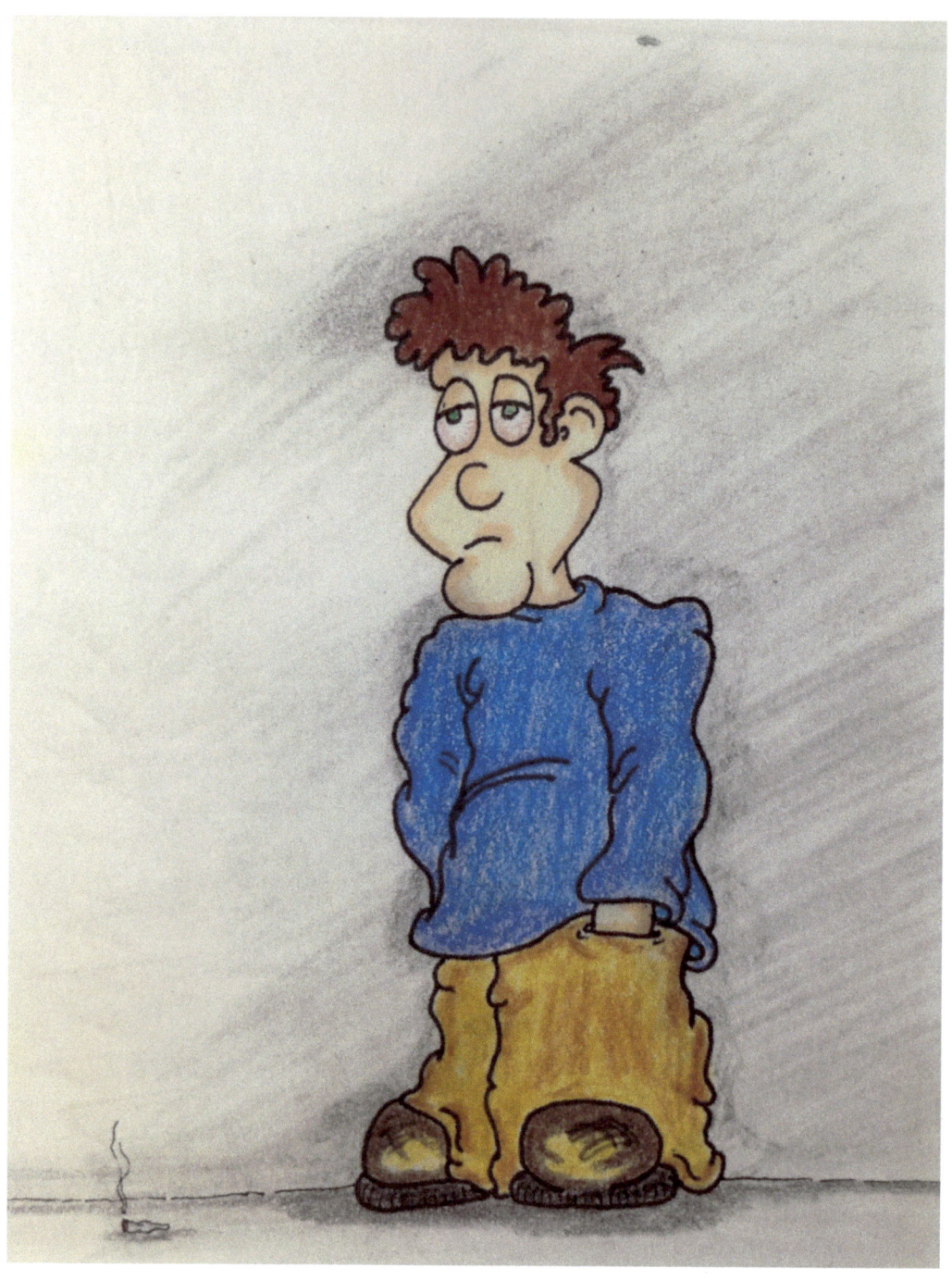

Feeling It — 1994 — 6 inches x 6 inches

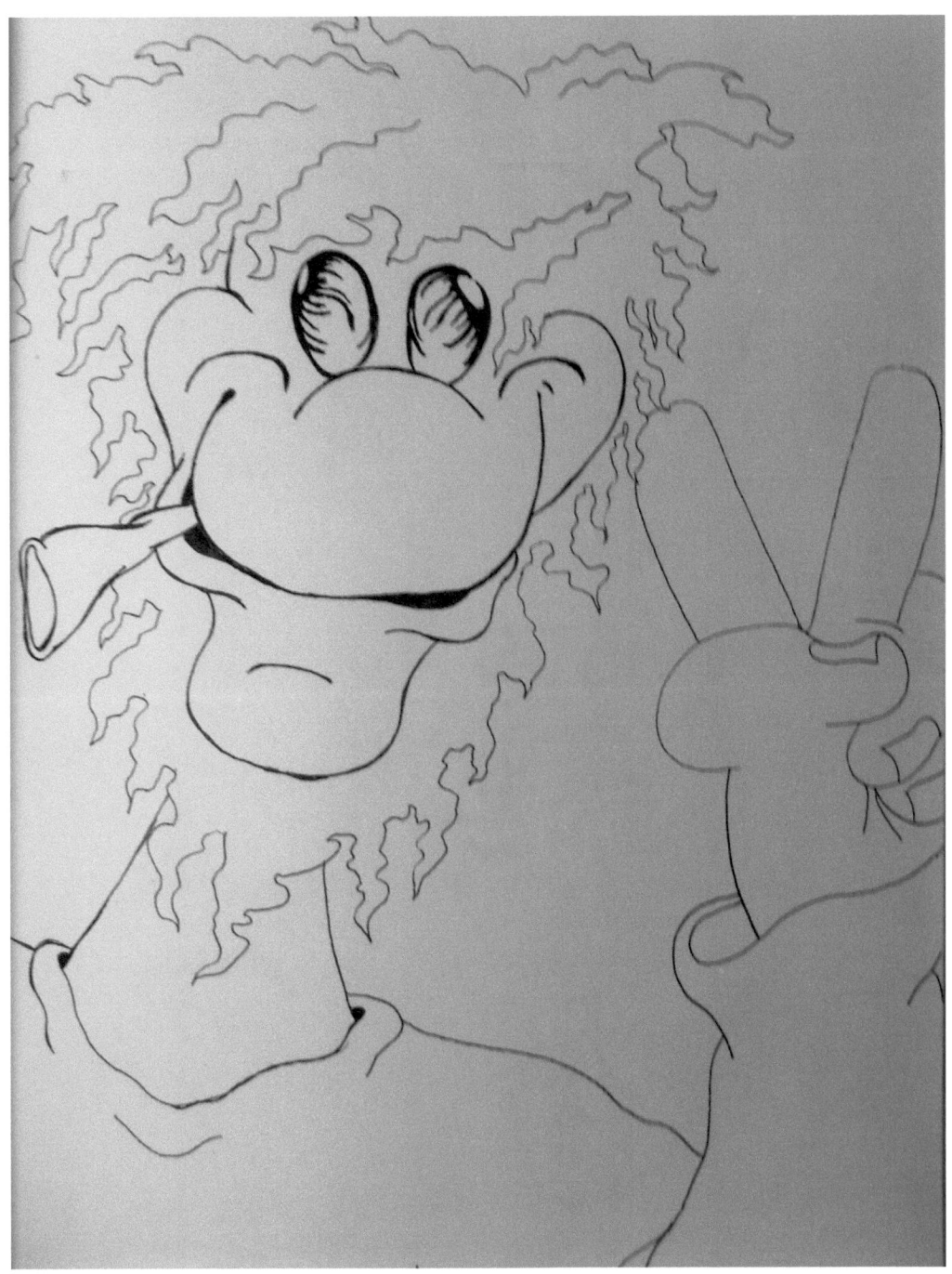

518 Late Night		1994		8 inches x 11 inches

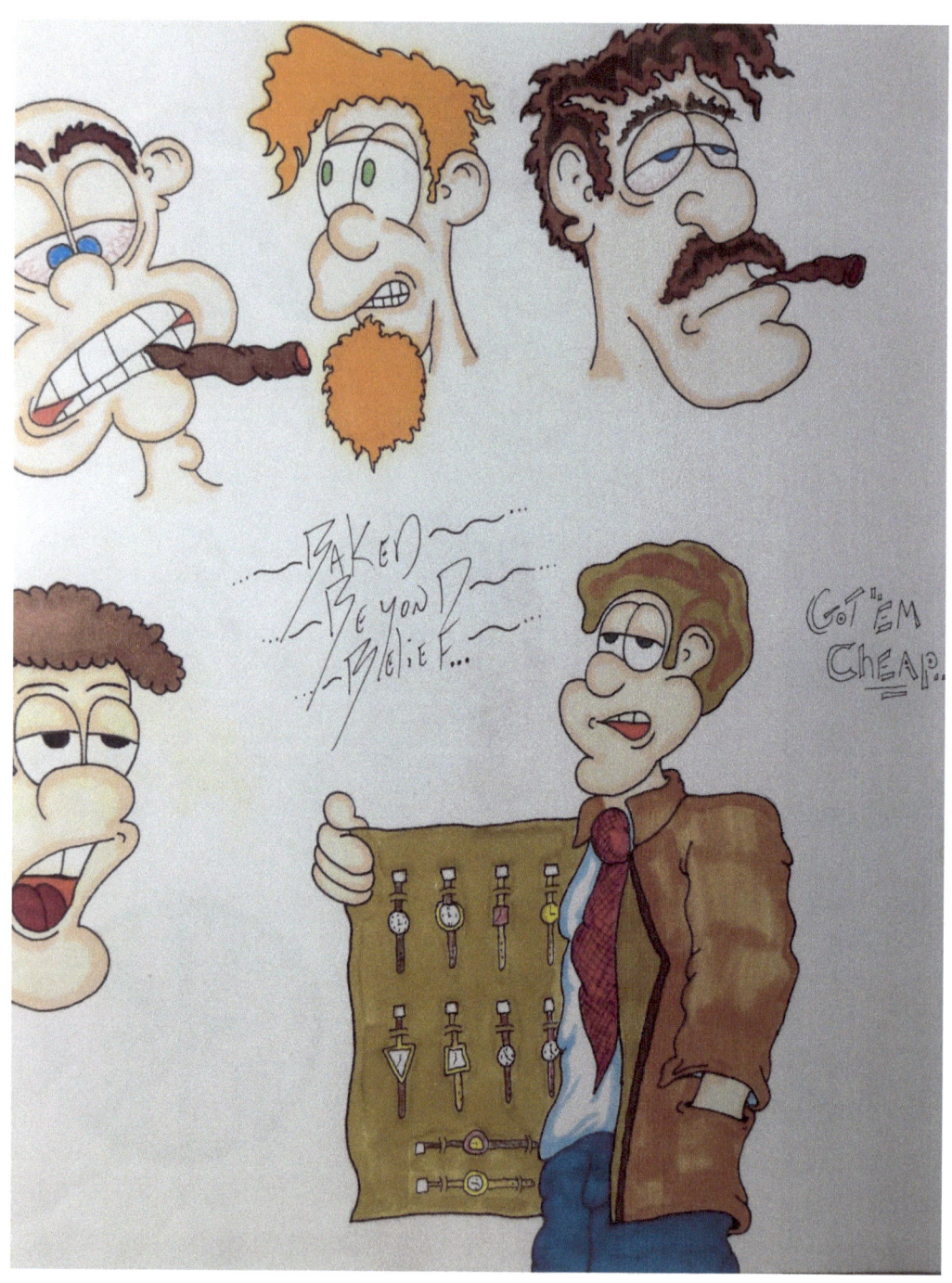

Faces with Got'Em Cheap — 1994 — 9 inches x 10 inches

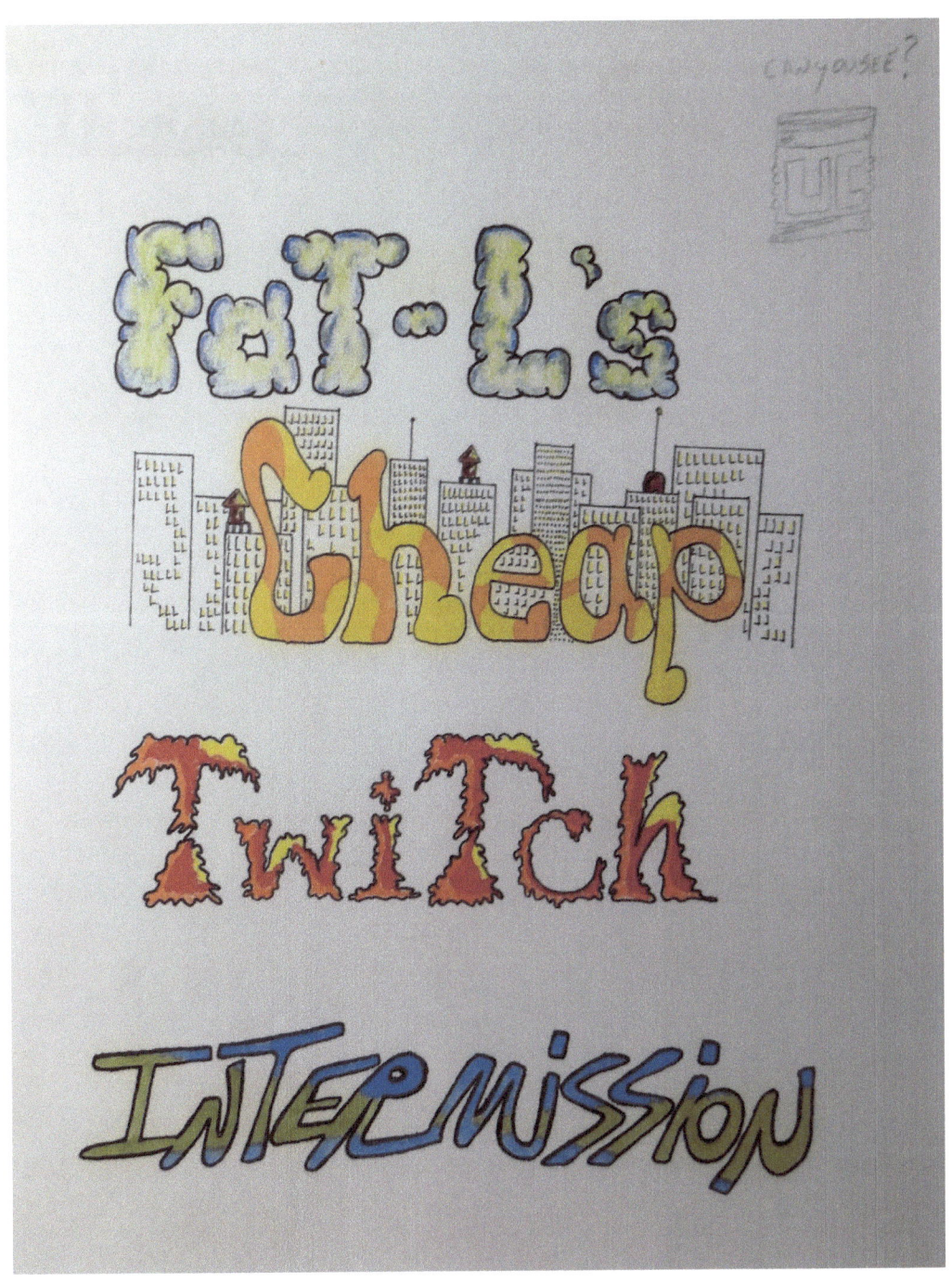

Can You See? 1994 8 inches x 9 inches

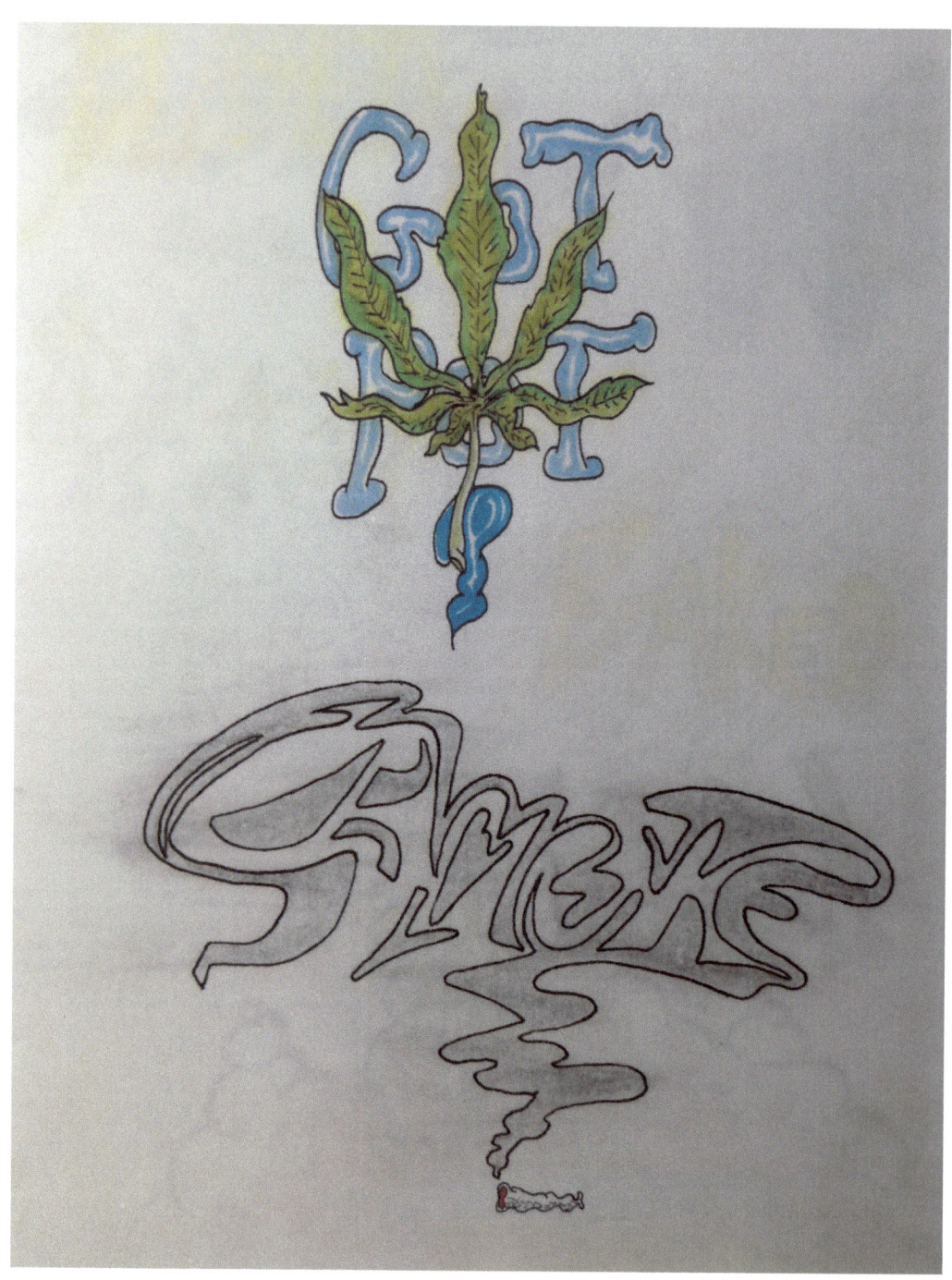

Got Pot Smoke In Smoke   1994   8 inches x 8 inches

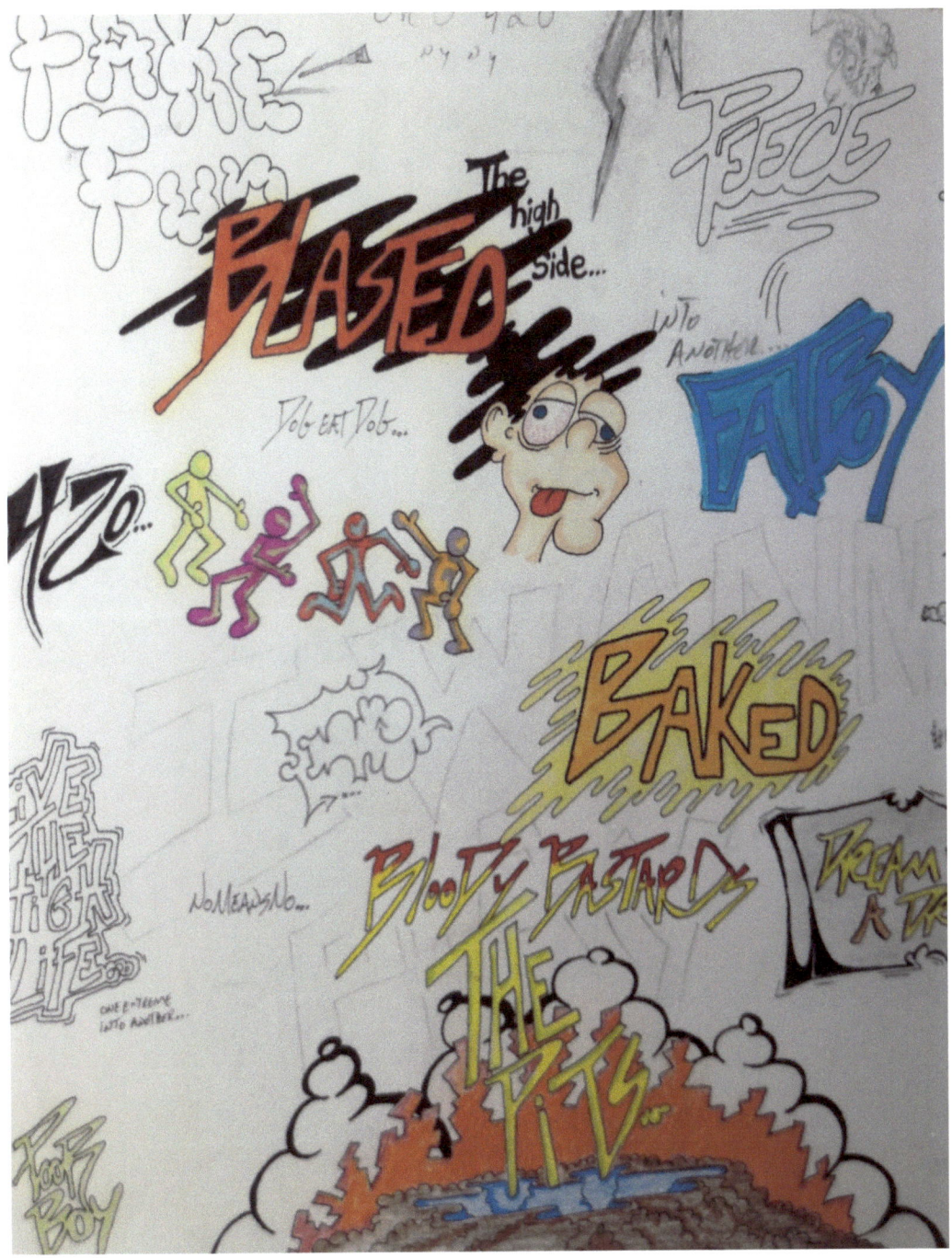

Just Doodling — 1994 — 9 inches x 10 inches

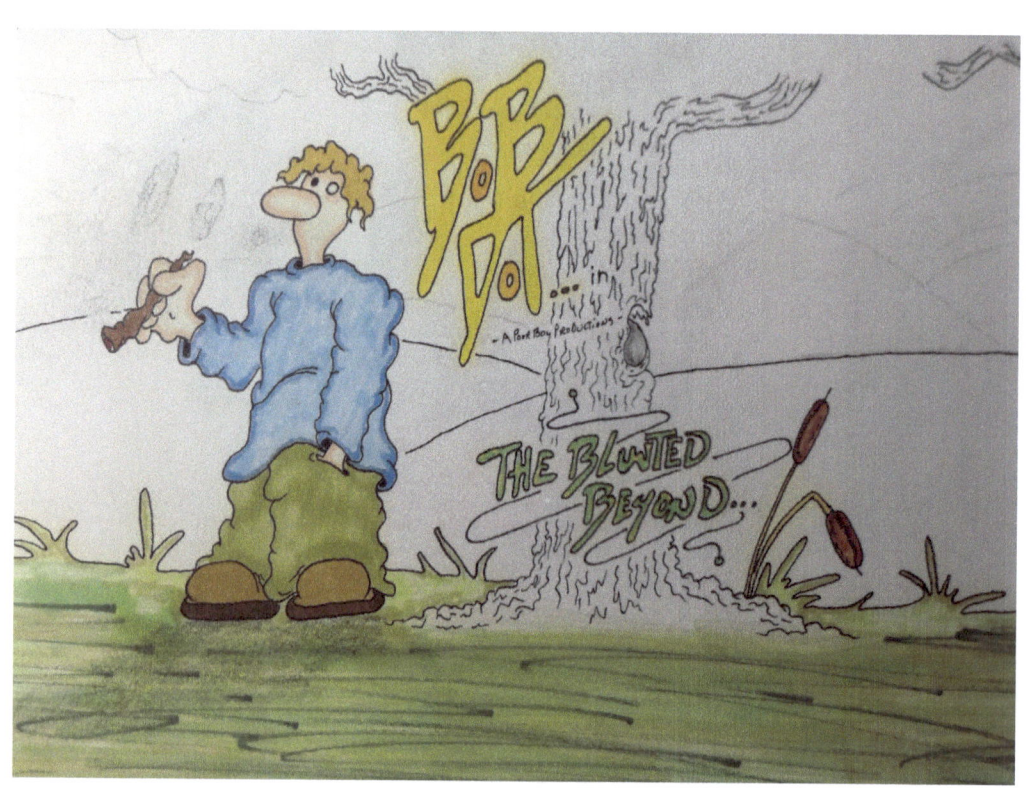

30 Page Lost Comic Strip 1994 10 inches x 9 inches

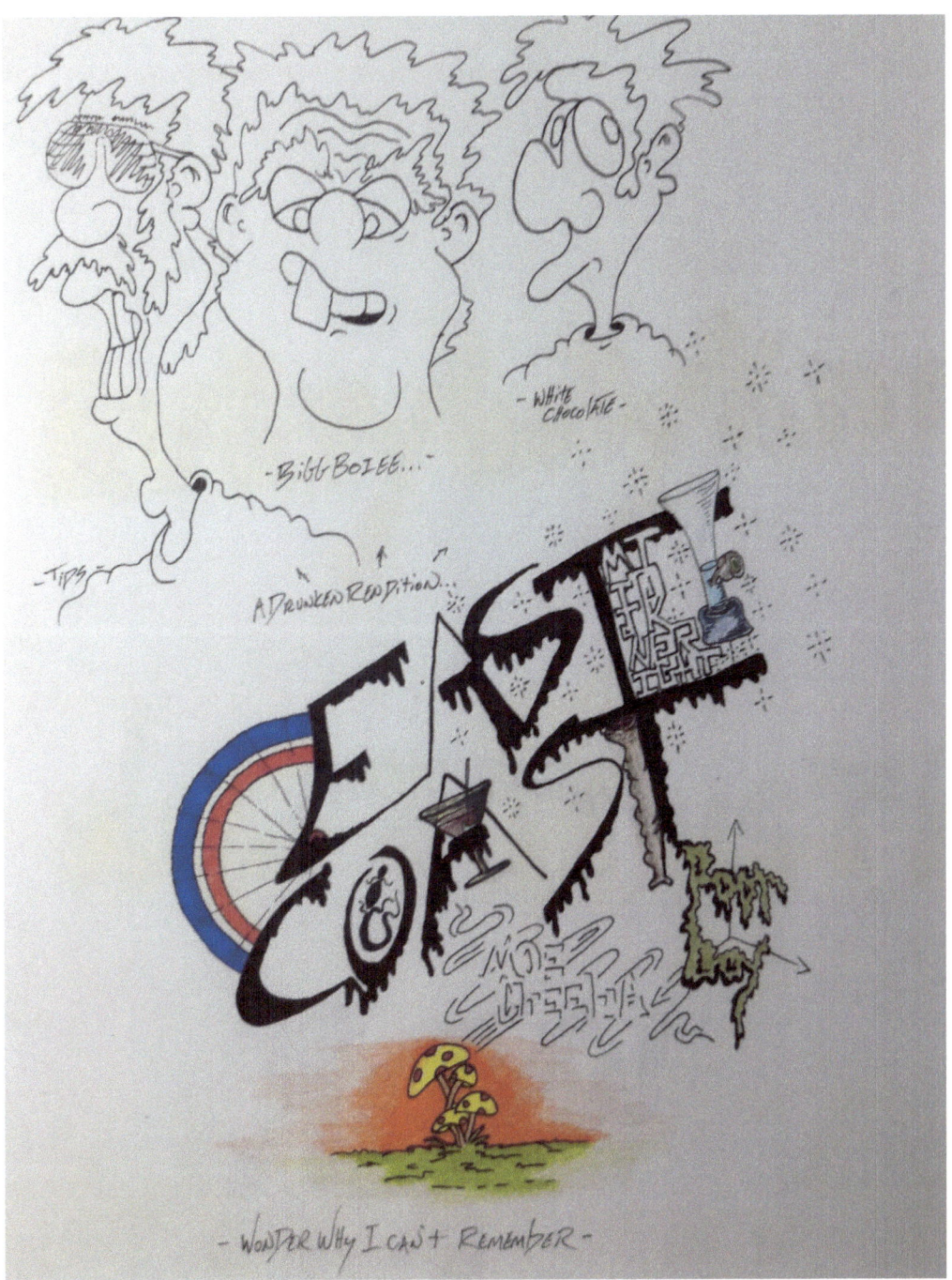

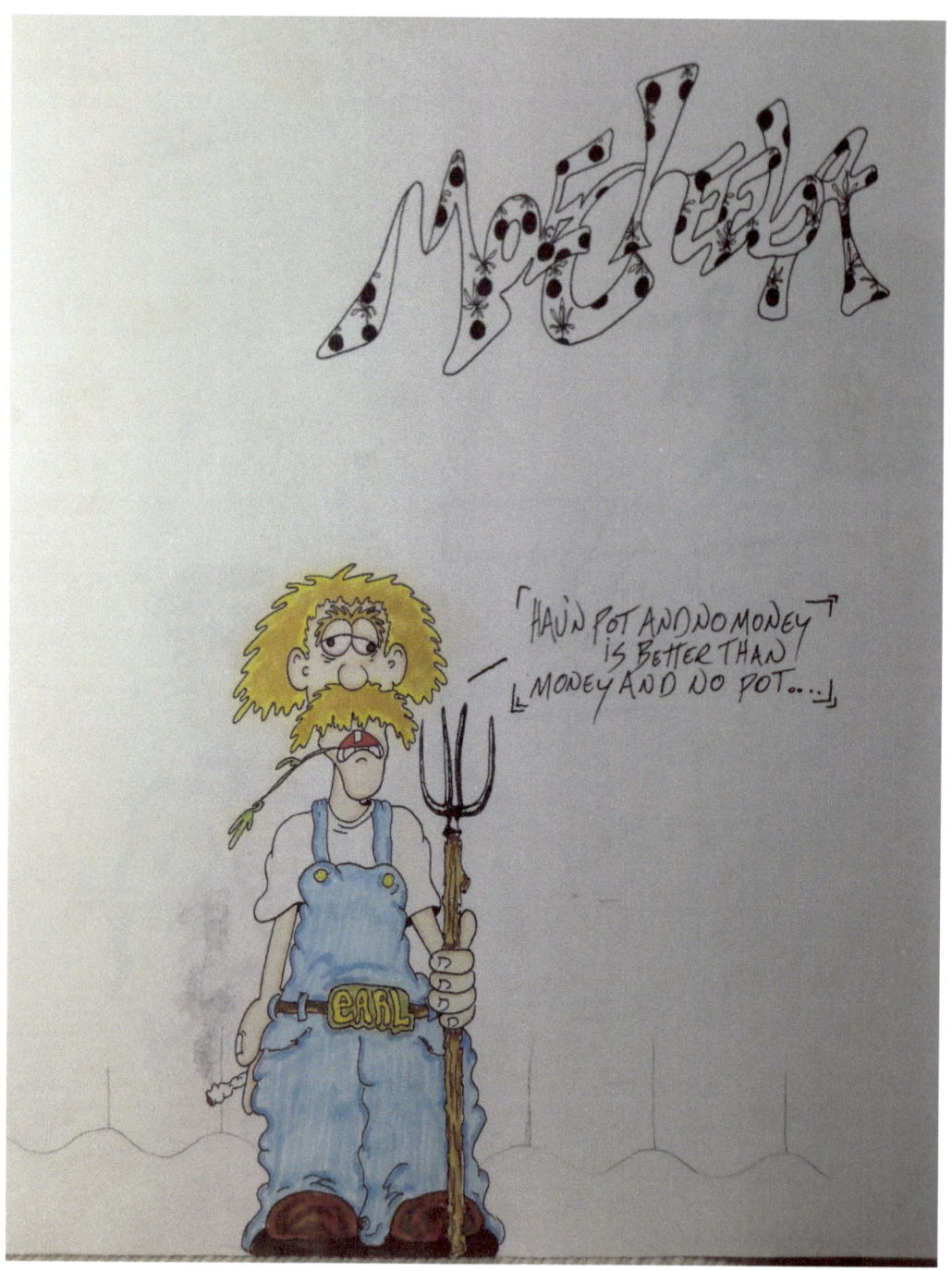

Moe Cheeba — 1994 — 9 inches x 10 inches

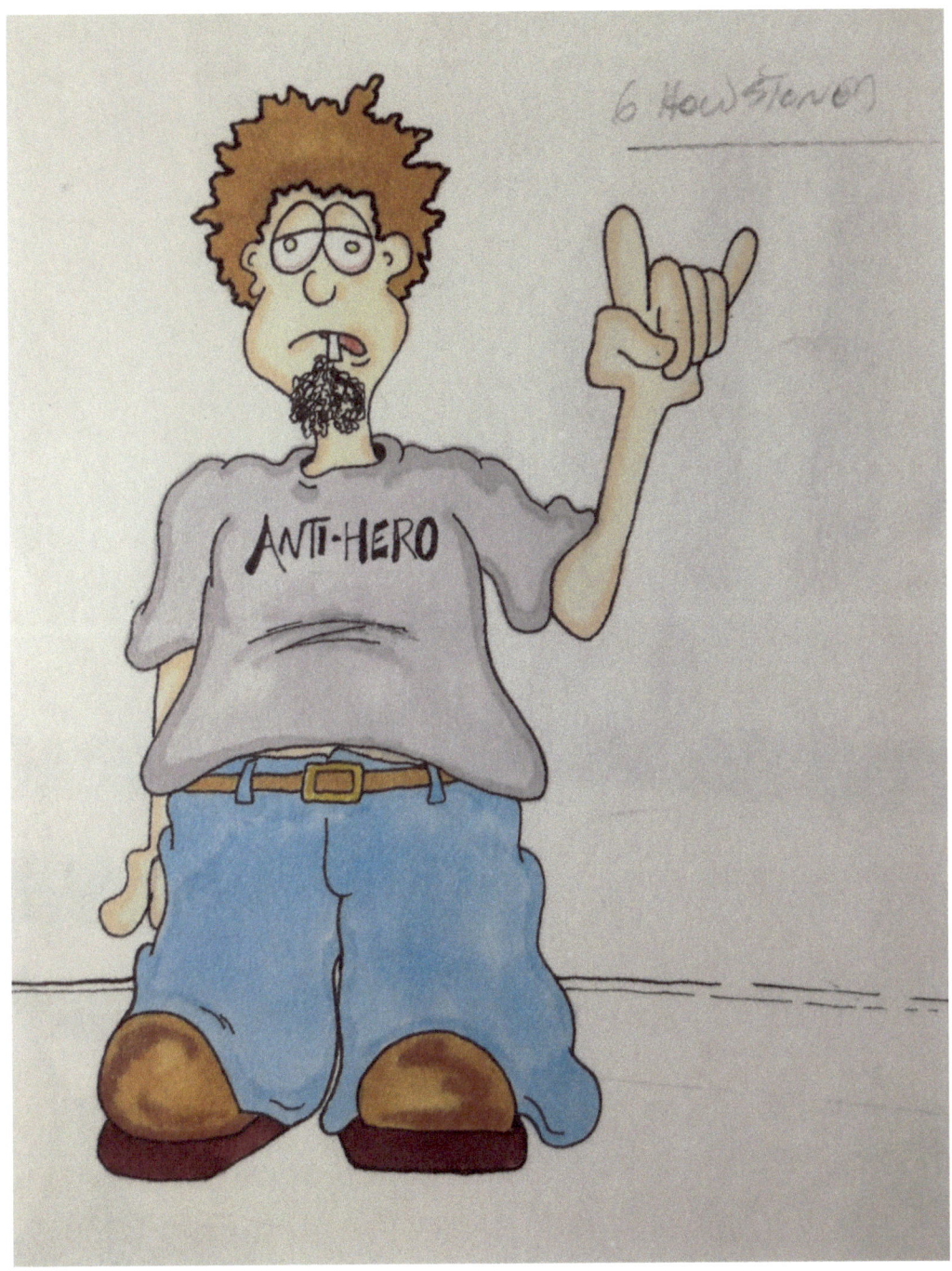

Anti-Hero   1994   5 inches x 5 inches

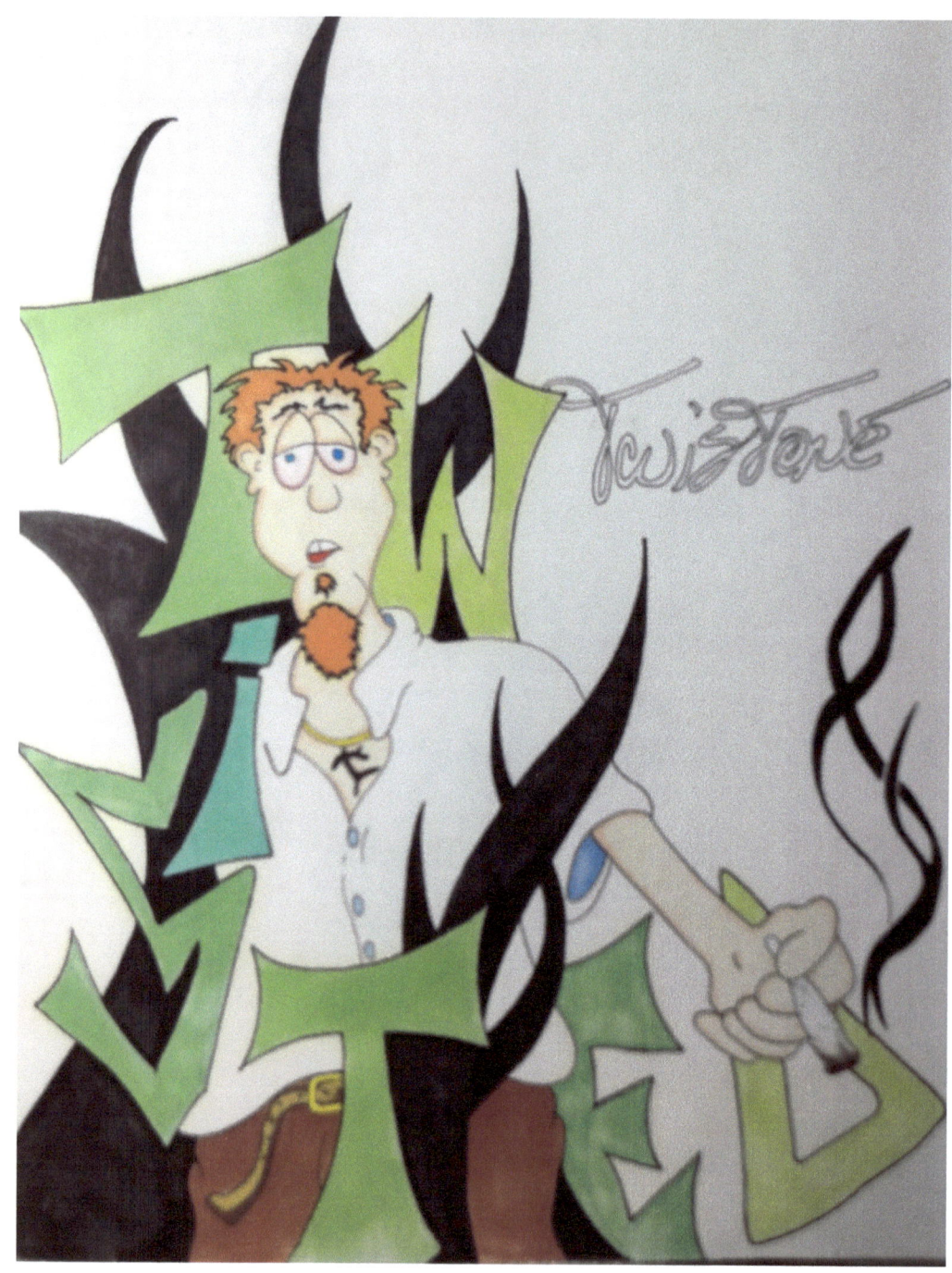

Twisted One   1994   9 inches x 10 inches

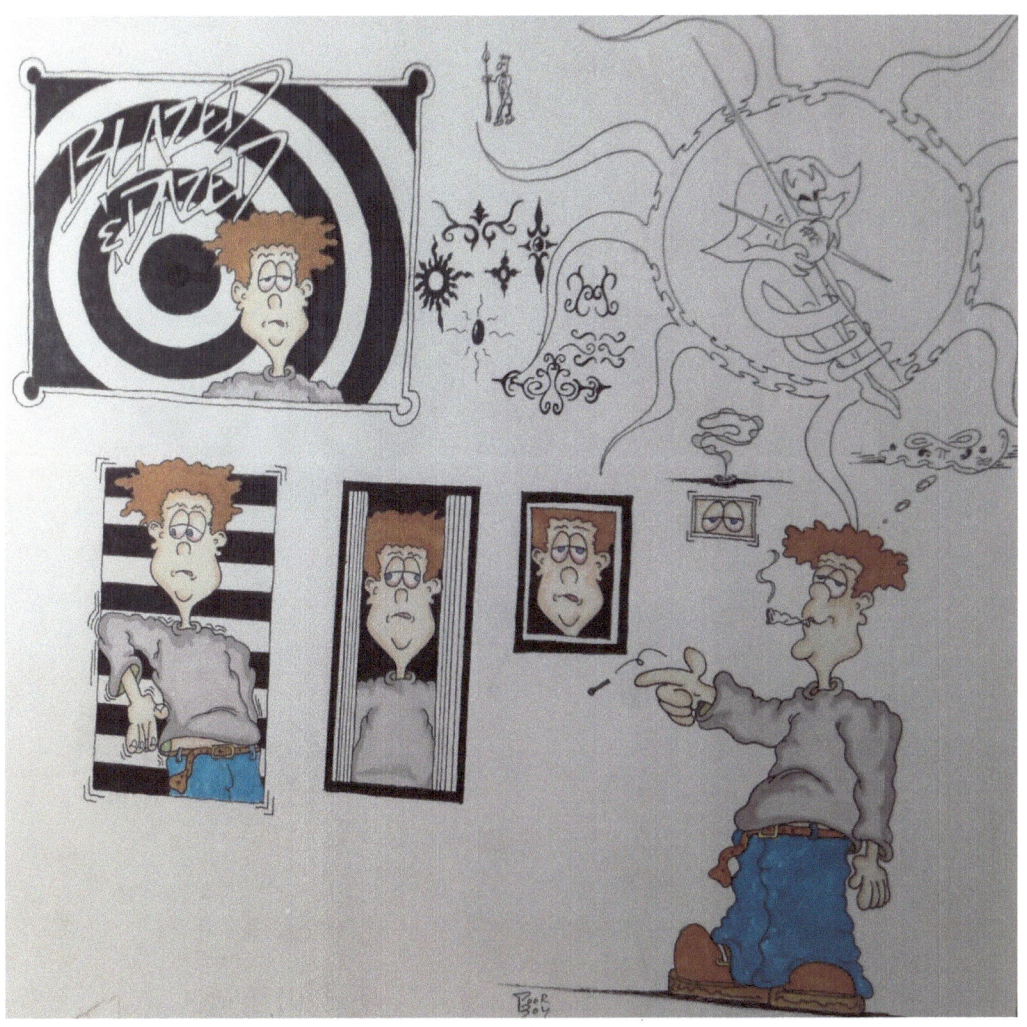

Guardian of the Nucleus — 1995 — 10 inches x 10 inches

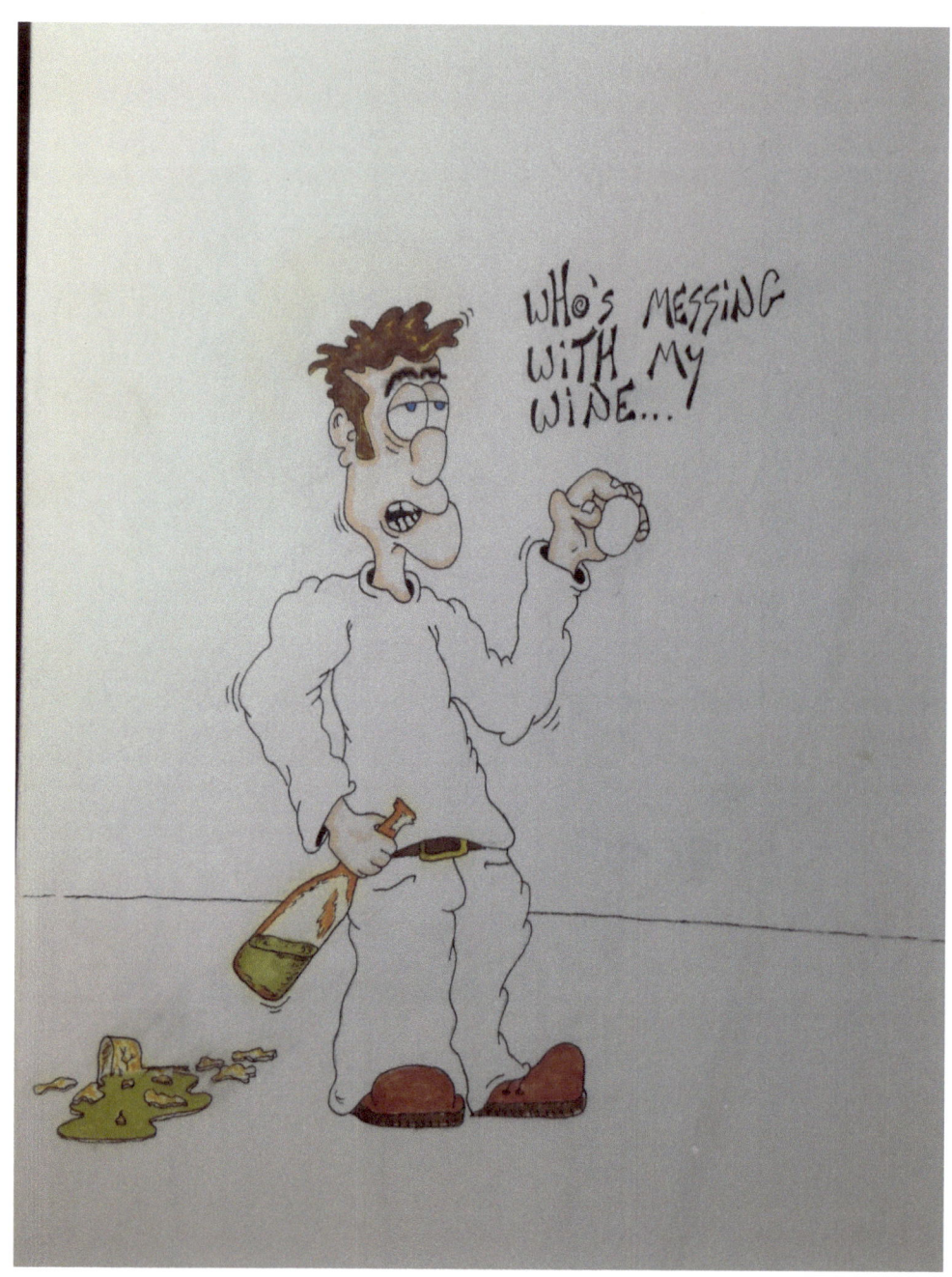

Wino Whining — 2010 — 7 inches x 8 inches

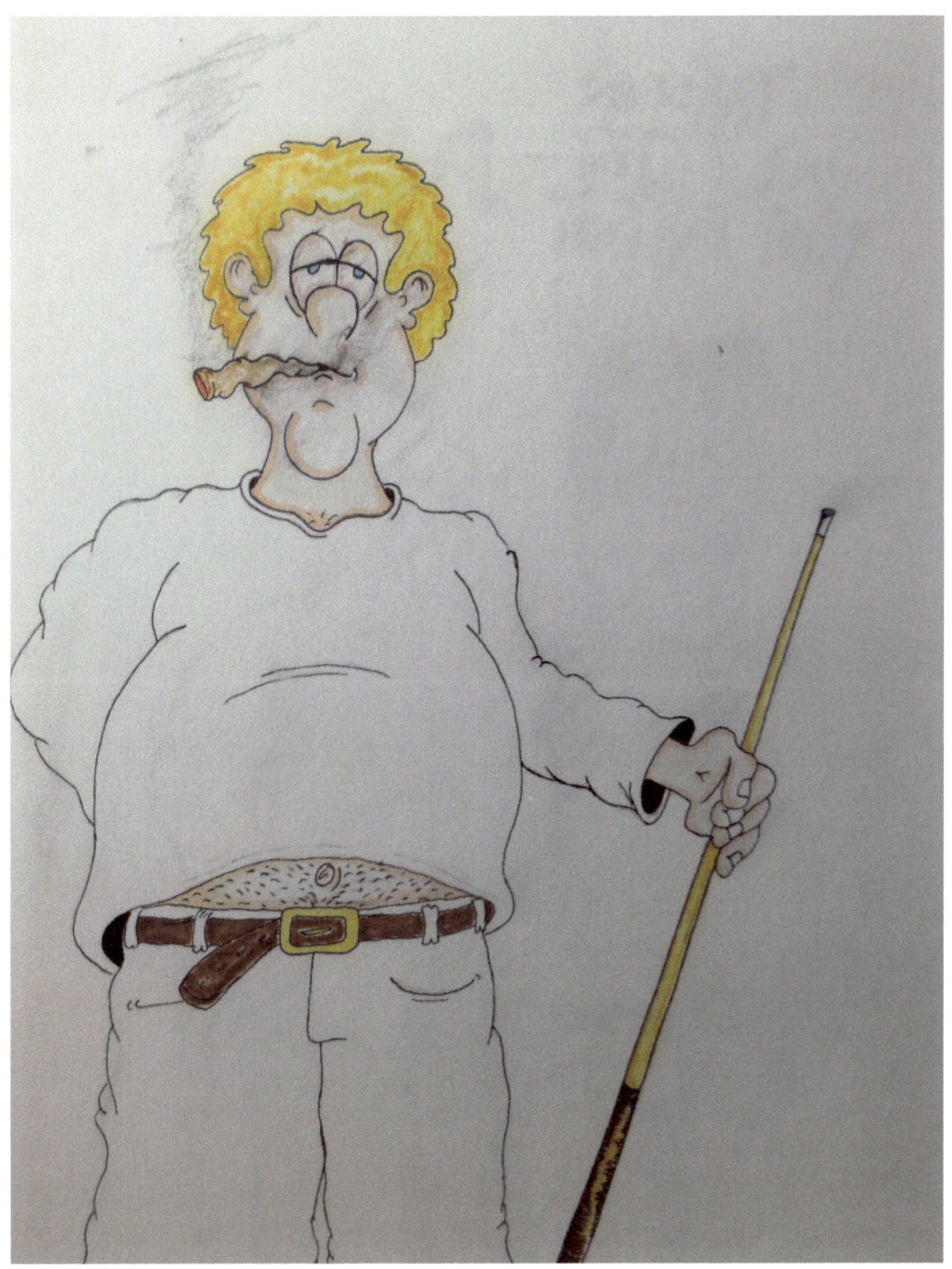

High or Low Balls — 2010 — 6 inches x 8 inches

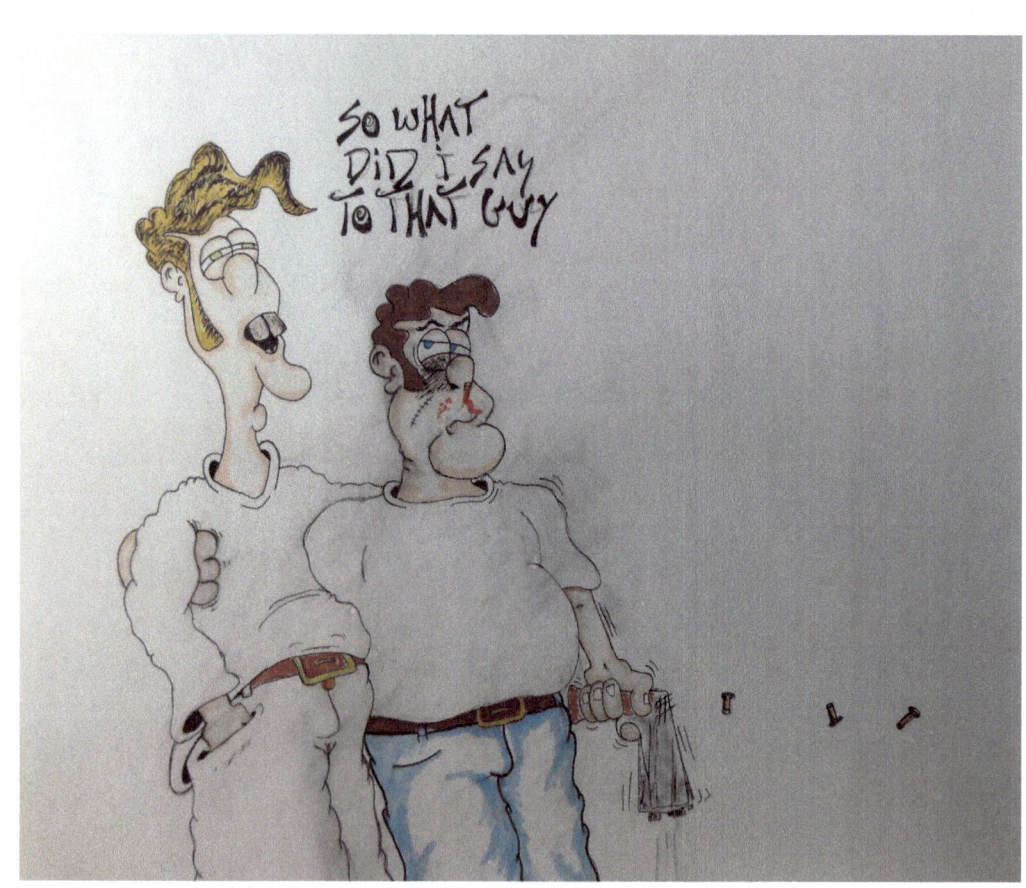

Watch What You Say — 2010 — 10 inches x 9 inches

I drew this after seeing them across the bridge at the local venue. They were great! Even after thirty or so years of attending shows there, being in the pit is never disappointing. Always a fun time there.

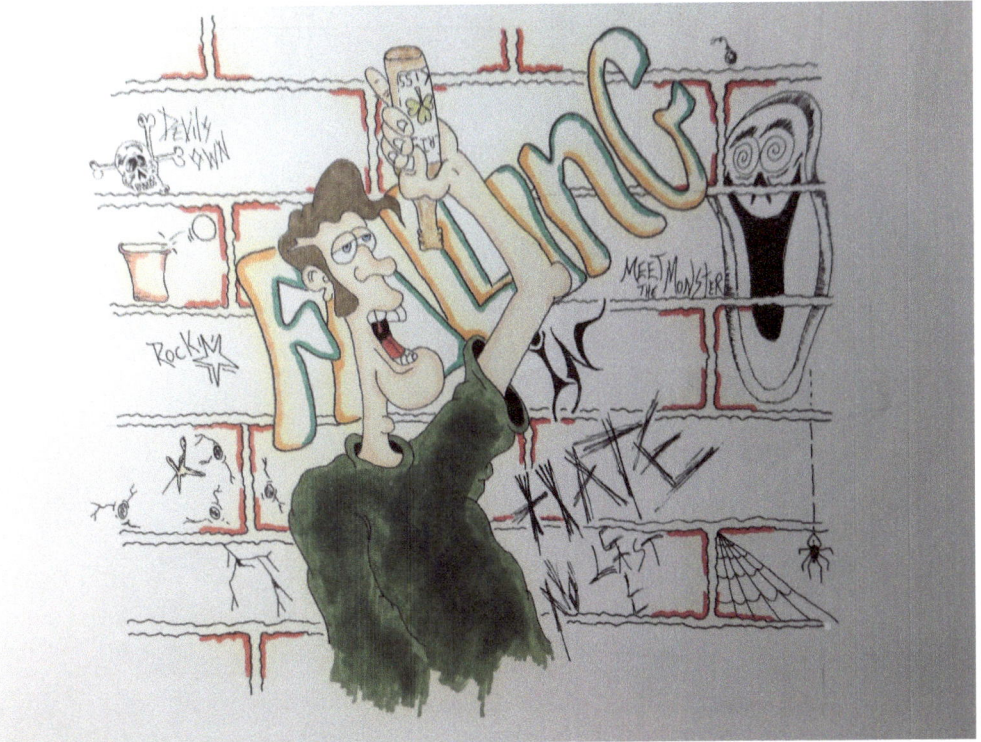

5 Finger Rock!   2010   8 inches x 8 inches

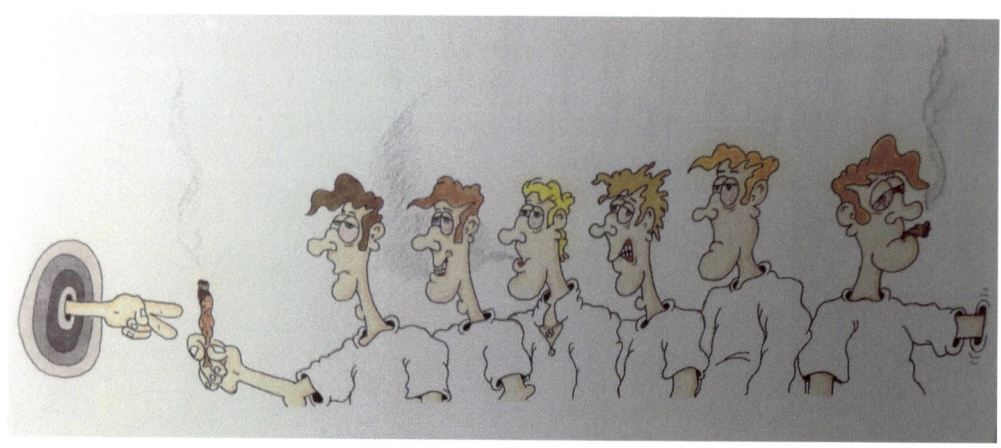

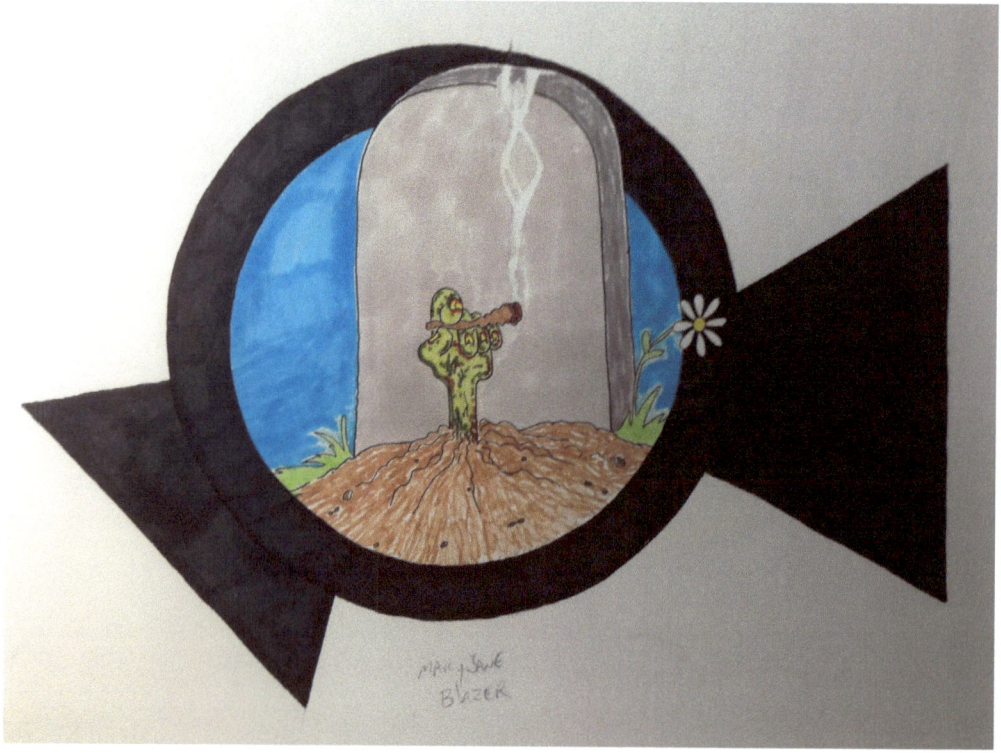

Puff, Puff Pass Portal   (top)   2011   11 inches x 5 inches
Last Pass   (bottom)   2012   11 inches x 8 inches

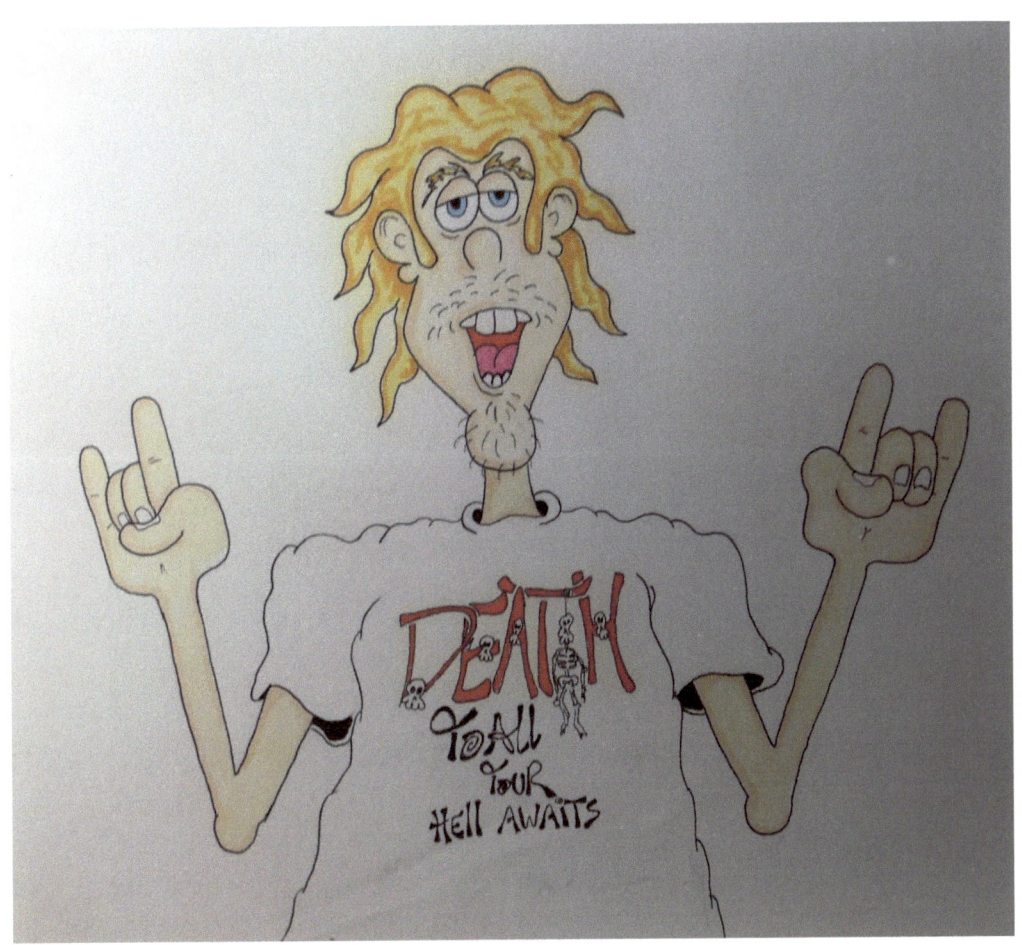

Going to the Show   2015   9 inches x 8 inches

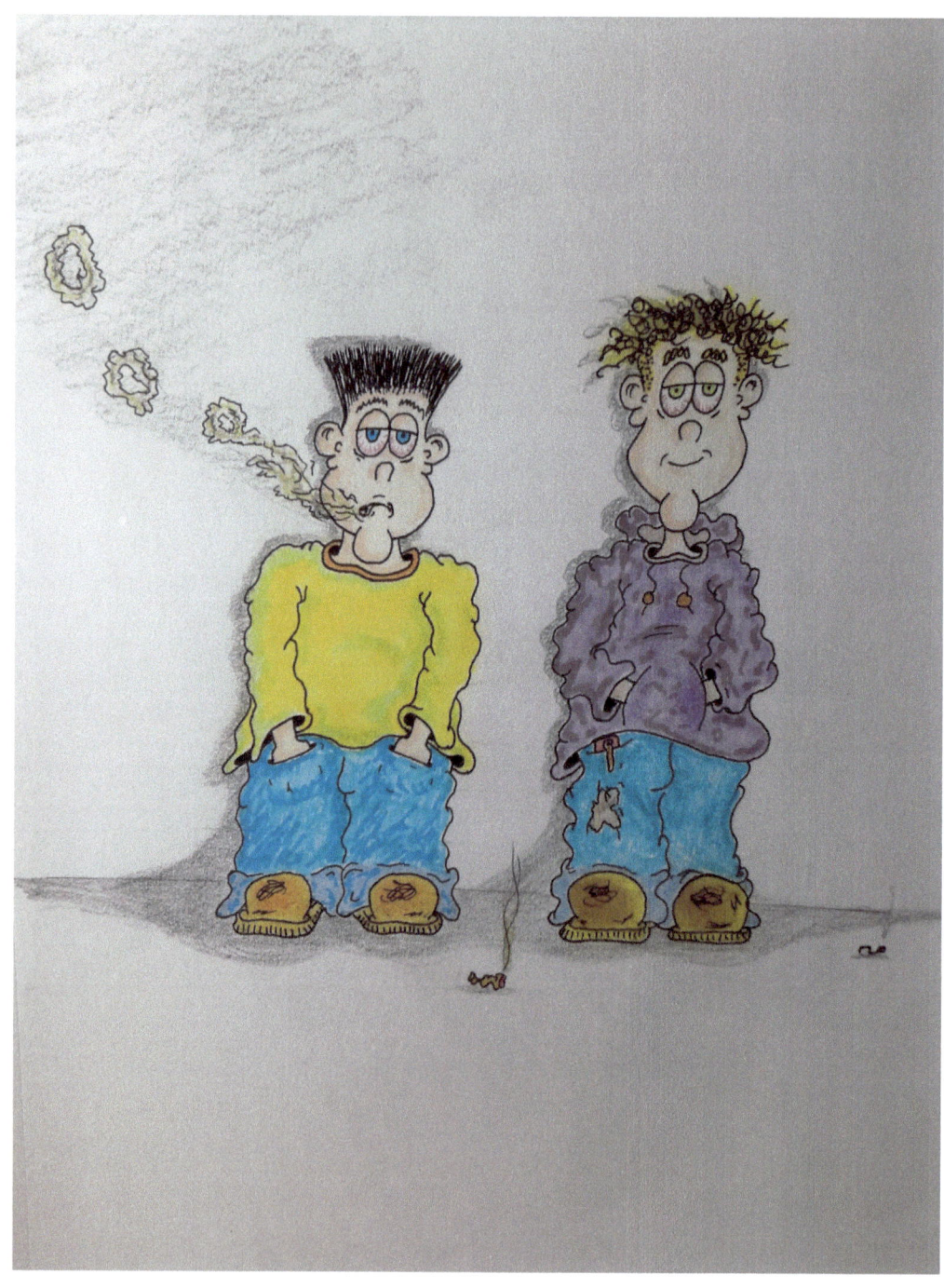

Got Five On It

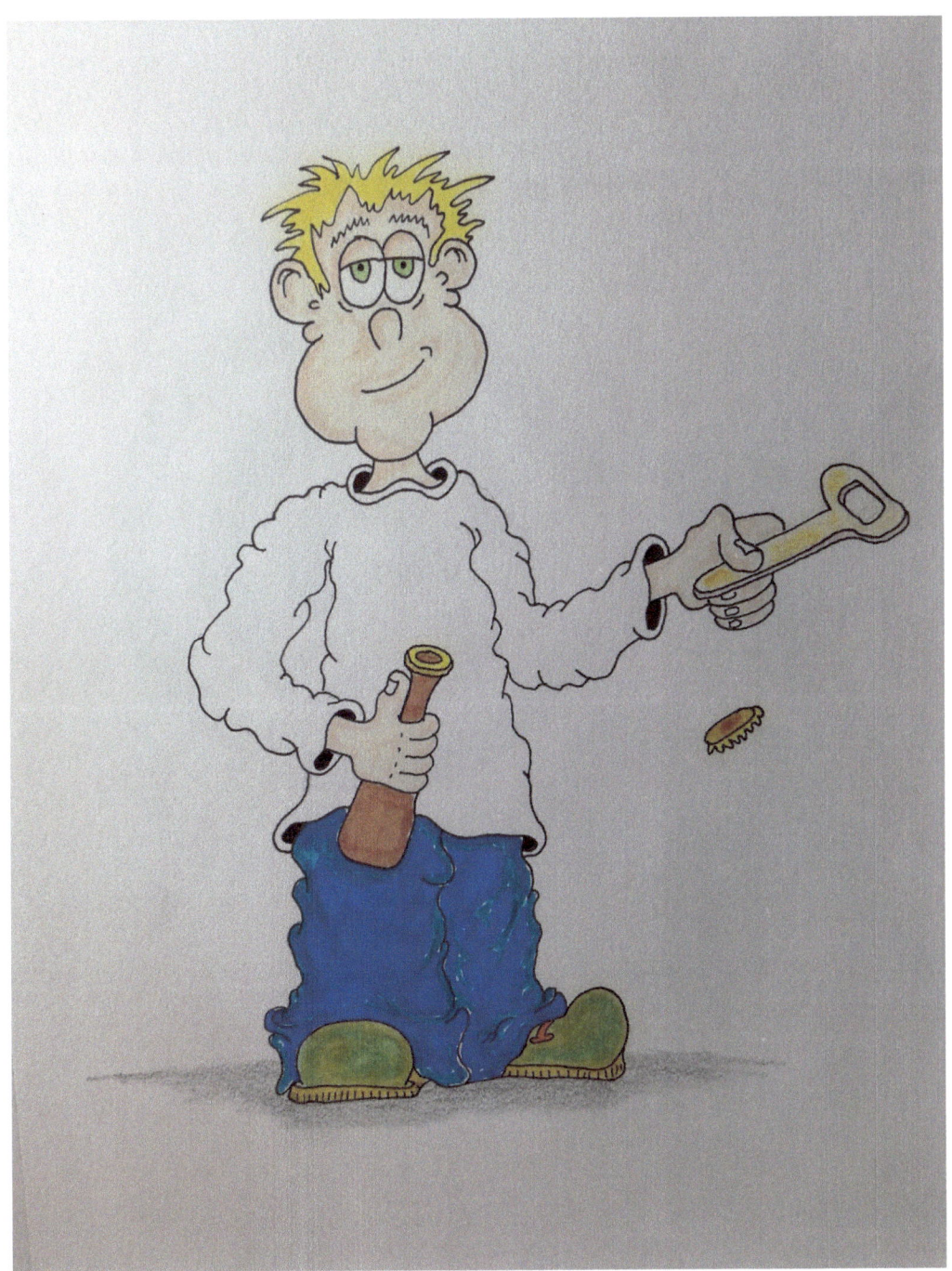

Excess in Moderation   2017   7 inches x 8 inches

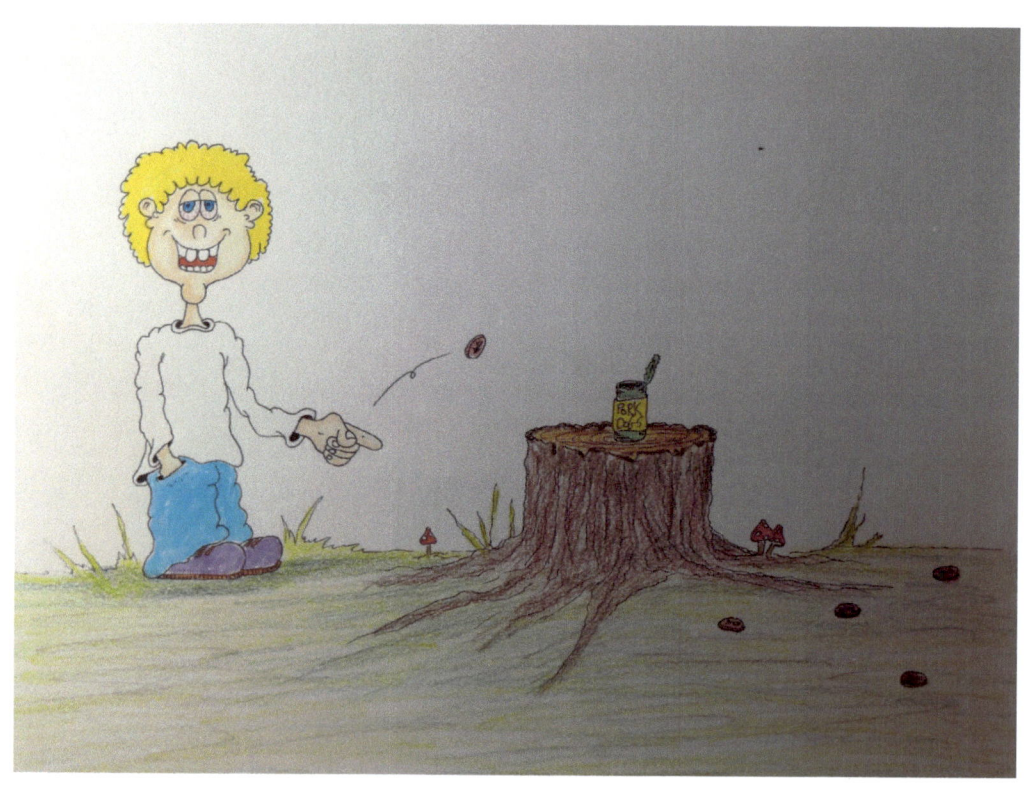

Annual Pork Dog Coin Toss   2017   11 inches x 8 inches

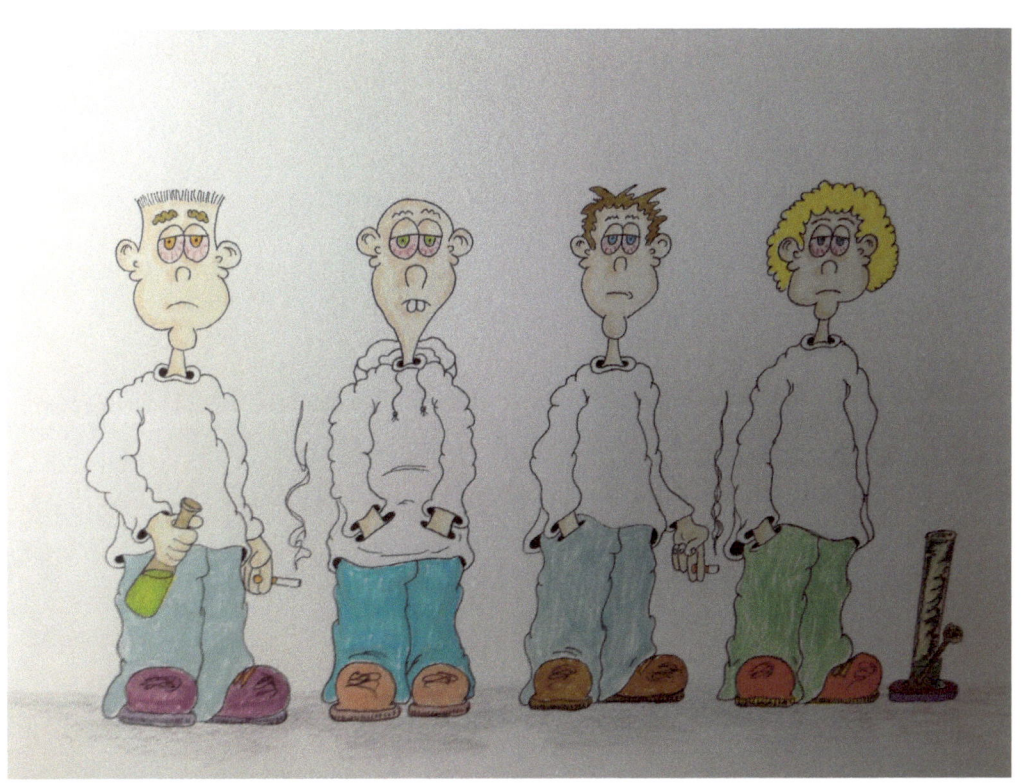

Party on Days That End With Y   2017   11 inches x 7 inches

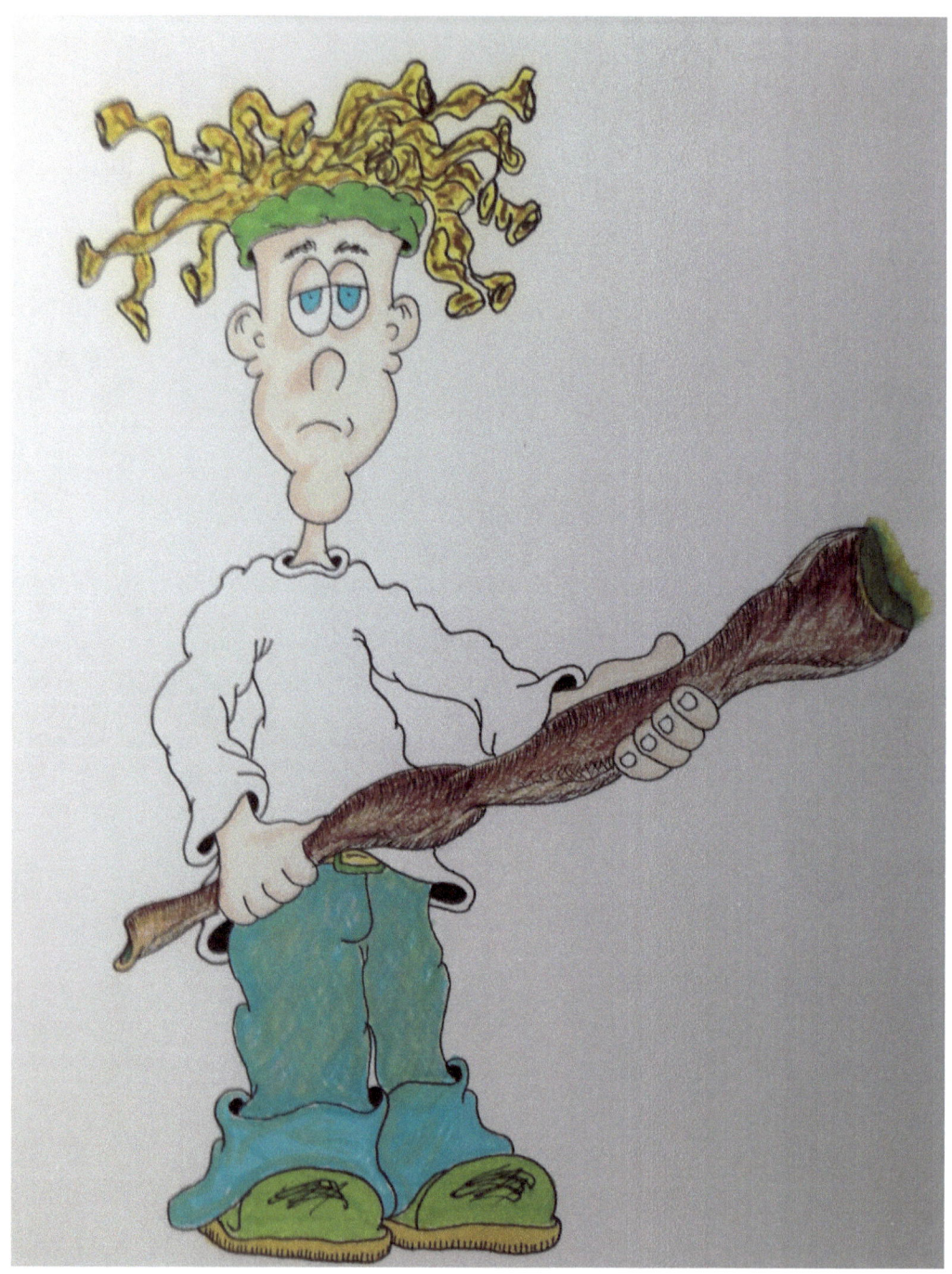

Bazooka Blunt — 2018 — 8 inches x 8 inches

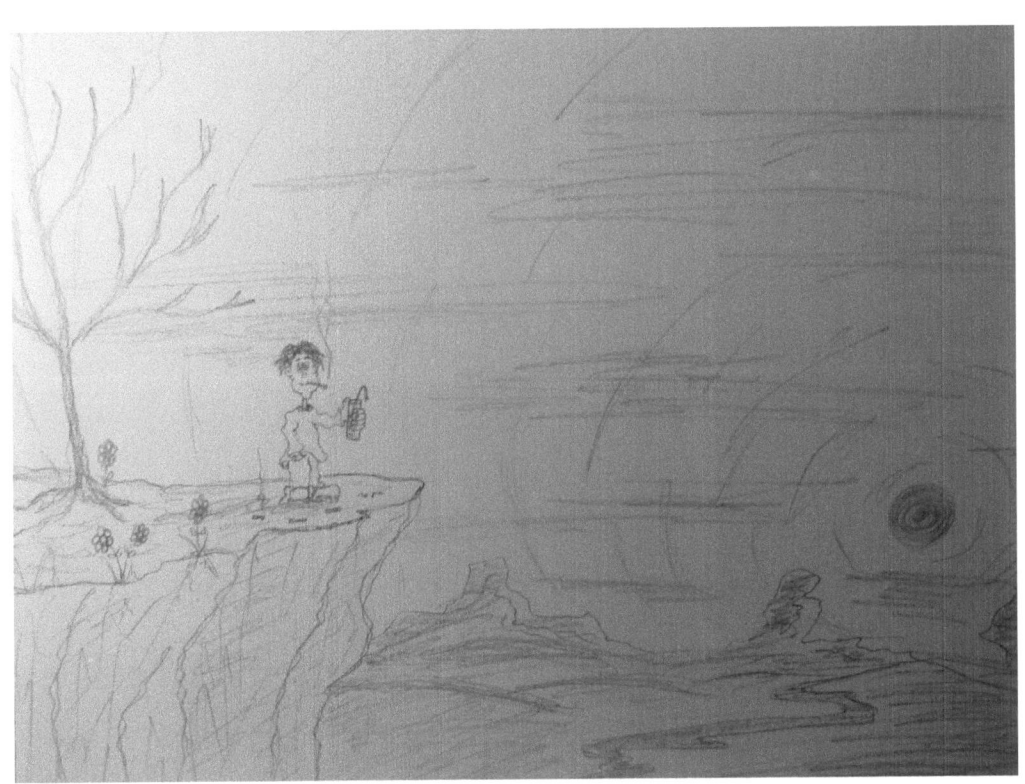

A Bunch of Nothing to Do   2018   11 inches x 8 inches

This is the first drawing in the most recent sketch book.

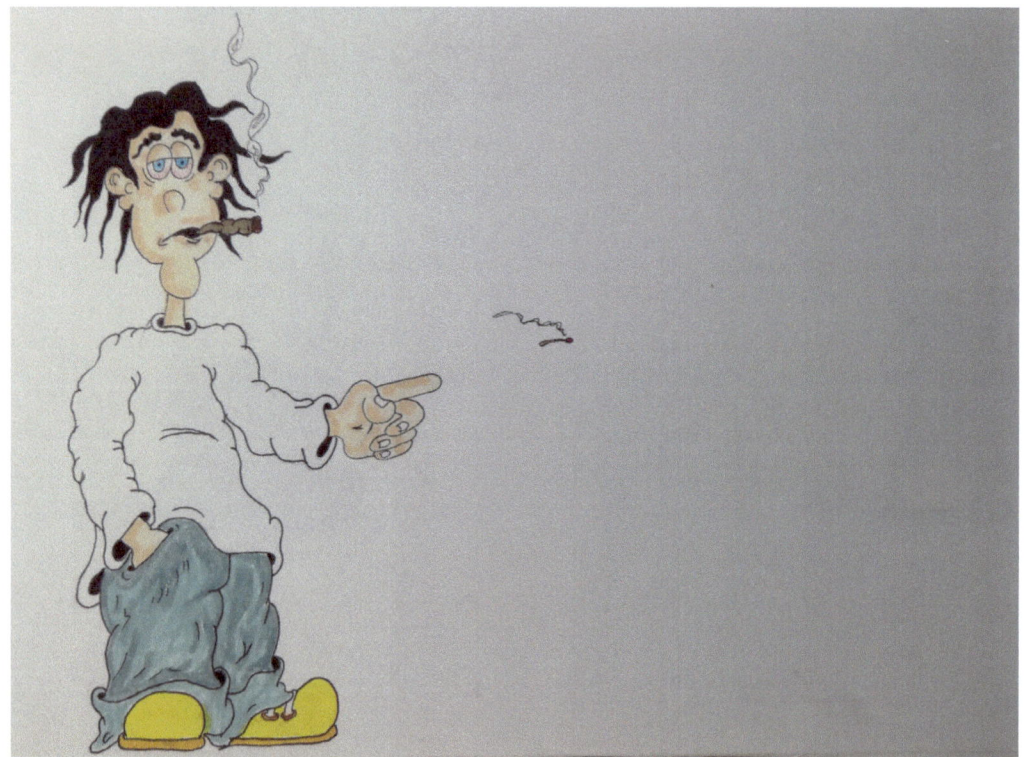

840 Twice the Fun   2018   7 inches x 8 inches

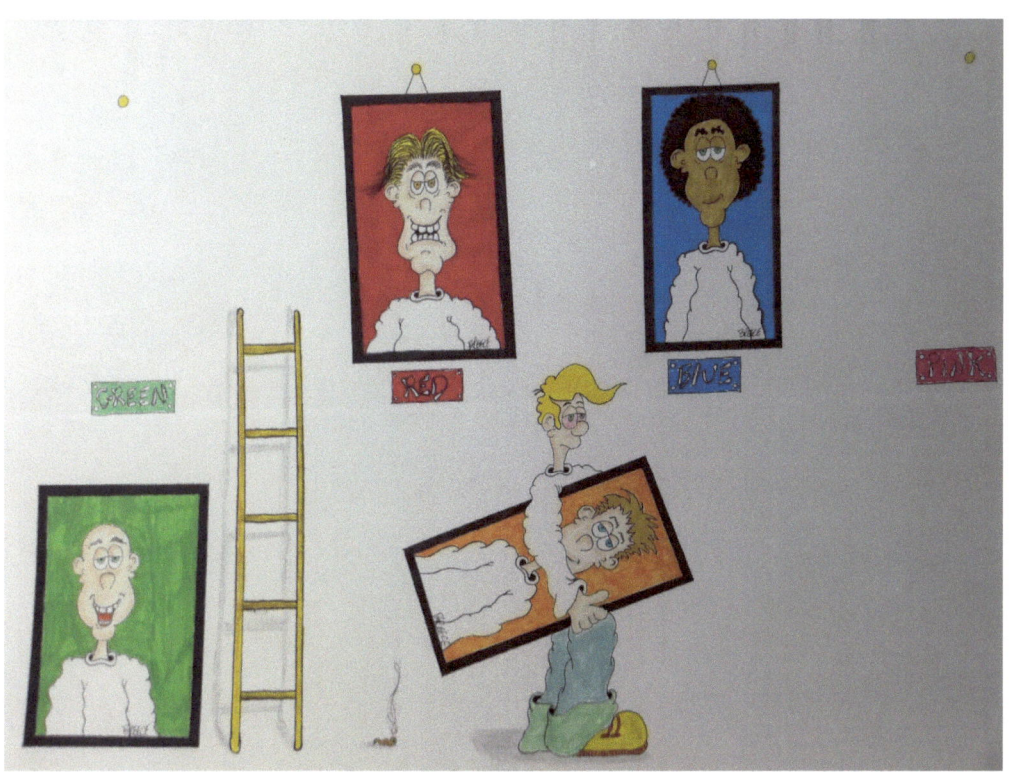

Color Blind 2018 14 inches x 11 inches

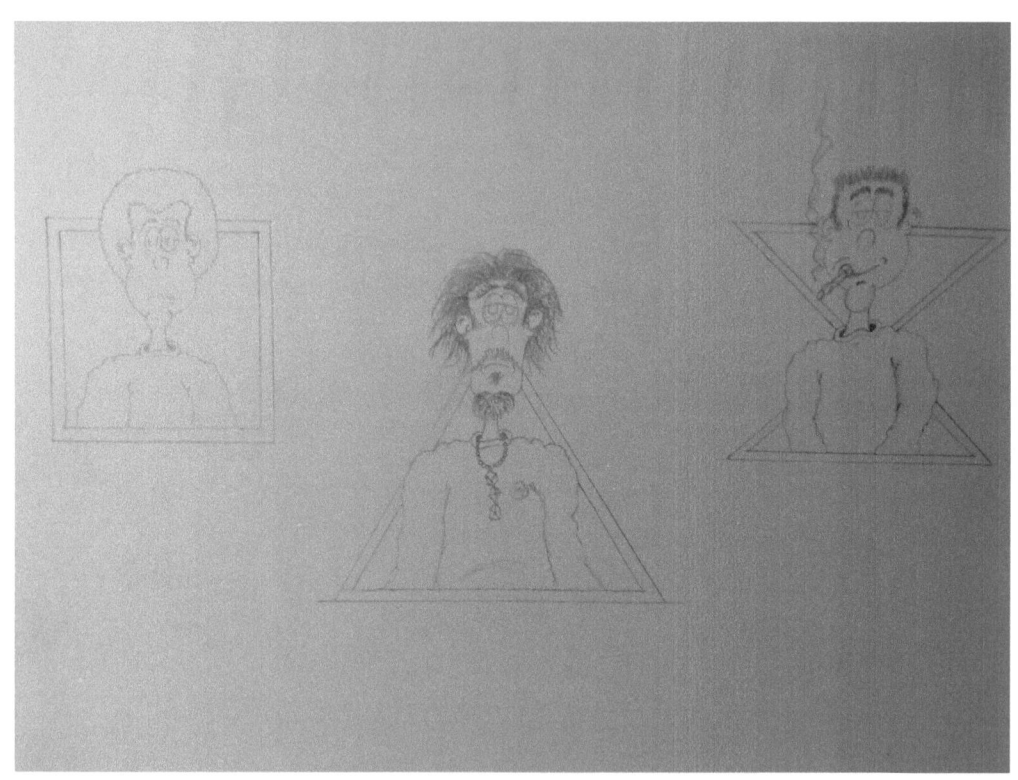

Unfinished Shape Up — 2018 — 14 inches x 8 inches

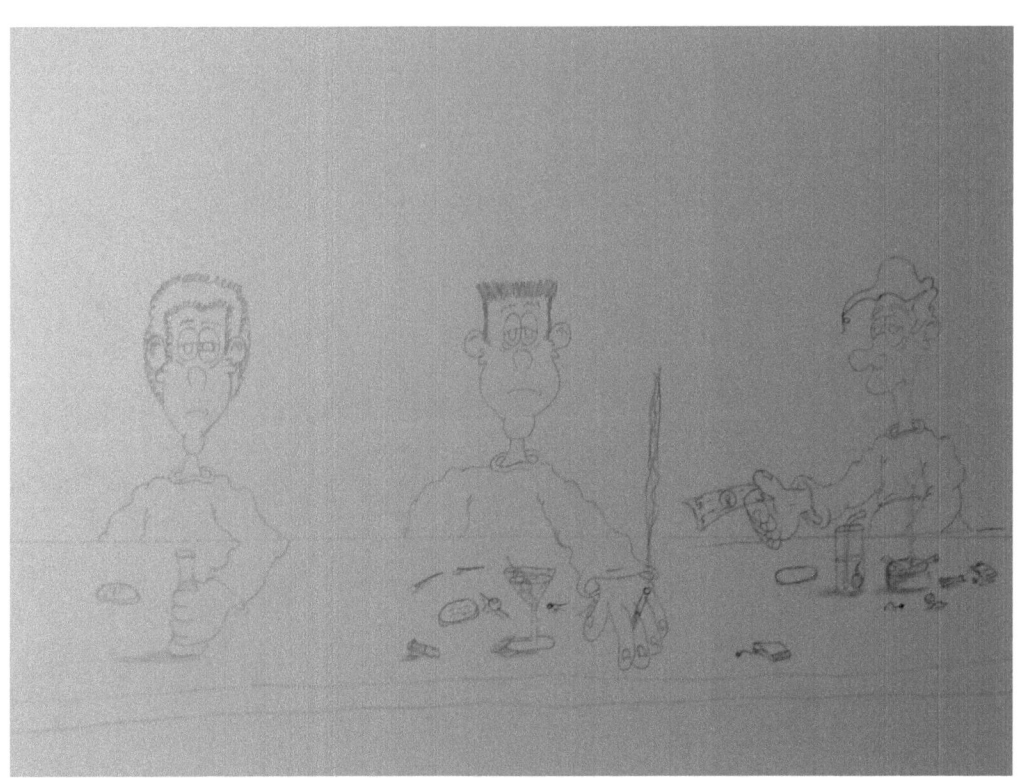

Unfinished Liquid Lunch   2018   14 inches x 10 inches

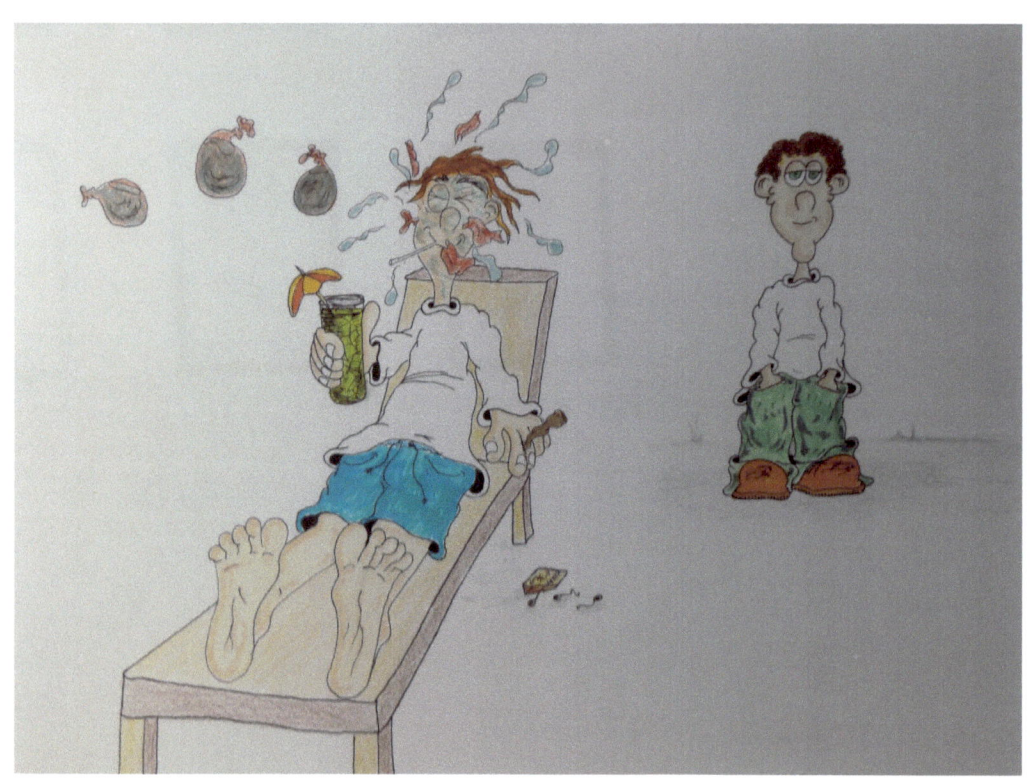

Just Sparked — 2019 — 12 inches x 9 inches

Thanks for making it to the end! Hope everyone has been entertained and has a smile. Remember, always have fun.
                                        Breece A. Perry

Index

Introduction	Age Restriction Warning	Page 2
Sun, Downed a Sixer		Page 3
Learning the Alphabet		Page 4
Out in Public		Page 5
*Nice		Page 6
*Hippy Metal		Page 7
*The Red Eye (top)	*Probably 4:19 (bottom)	Page 8
*BongBoy		Page 9
Trench Lighter		Page 10
Broken Ankle		Page 11
Black Light and Blue (top)	Need a Teammate (bottom)	Page 12
Get'n High		Page 13
Lets Hang Out		Page 14
Bob Dot Feeling Blue		Page 15
Morning Glory		Page 16
New TV Remote		Page 17
Stoned Solid Grey		Page 18
PoorBoy		Page 19
Feeling It		Page 20
518 Late Night		Page 21
Faces with Got'Em Cheap		Page 22
Can You See?		Page 23
Got Pot Smoke In Smoke		Page 24
Just Doodling		Page 25
30 Page Lost Comic Strip		Page 26
Morning, College Departure		Page 27
Moe Cheeba		Page 28
Anti-Hero		Page 29
Twisted One		Page 30
Guardian of the Nucleus		Page 31
Wino Whining		Page 32
High or Low Balls		Page 33
Watch What You Say		Page 34
5 Finger Rock!		Page 35
Puff, Puff Pass Portal (top)	Last Pass (bottom)	Page 36
Going to the Show		Page 37
Got Five On It		Page 38
Excess in Moderation		Page 39
Annual Pork Dog Coin Toss		Page 40
Party on Days That End With Y		Page 41
Bazooka Blunt		Page 42
A Bunch of Nothing to Do		Page 43
840 Twice the Fun		Page 44
Color Blind		Page 45
Unfinished Shape Up		Page 46
Unfinished Liquid Lunch		Page 47
Just Sparked		Page 48
Conclusion: Artist/ Author Sentiments		Page 49

www.ingramcontent.com/pod-product-compliance
Lightning Source LLC
Chambersburg PA
CBHW051219220526
45473CB00003B/1096